Edward H. Hutchins
New York City - May '86

Techniques of fund-raising

Techniques of fund-raising

DANIEL LYNN CONRAD
President, The Institute for Fund-Raising

Lyle Stuart, Inc./Secaucus, New Jersey

Published by Lyle Stuart, Inc.

Manufactured in the United States of America
ISBN 0-8184-0169-9

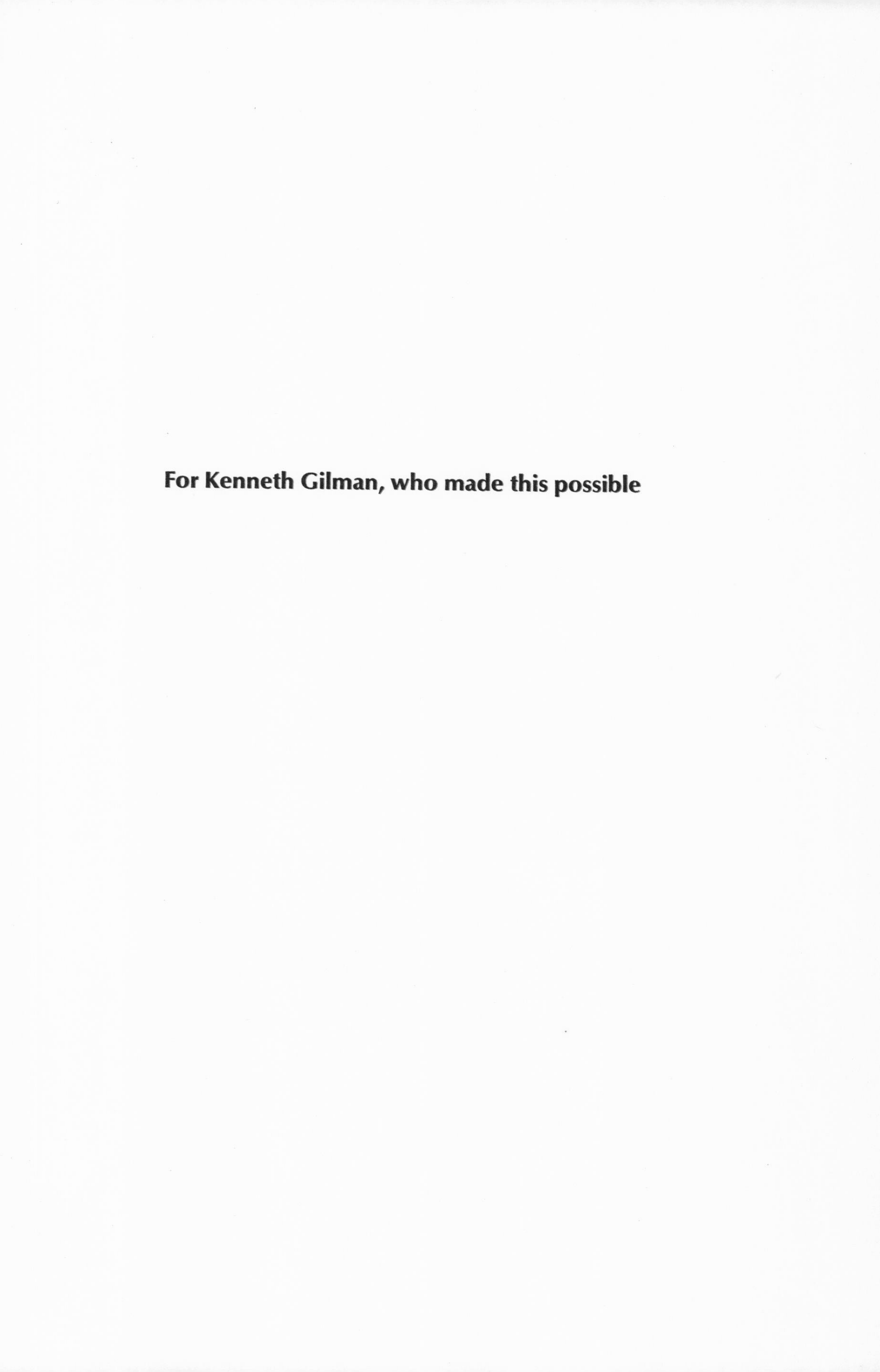

For Kenneth Gilman, who made this possible

Contents

Preface

Why don't charities dream more?

If I could change just one thing in charities today, I'd like them to dream more. Because dreaming is where great projects start.

In the course I teach, called "Techniques of Fund-Raising," I have been startled to discover only 10 to 20 per cent of the students have a written long-range or five-year plan. I don't understand this. The only way you ever get anything done is by setting a goal and making plans to reach it. To me, the reason charities don't raise more money is that they don't plan. And I think the reason they don't plan is that they don't dream.

Many non-profit organizations today are concerned with simply maintaining the status quo, not with how they could grow. This is a mistake, because I think the only way for organizations to survive is to grow. The reason is that charities are problem-solving institutions that try to meet the needs of society, and the needs of society will not remain the same for very long. You must do your best to try to keep up with society's needs. To repeat, charities will survive only if they grow.

Many charities will want to use this book to learn survival techniques. Instead, I hope you'll use it to find new ways of getting new money for new projects. In a sense, it should be called *How to Raise Money to Ful-*

fill Your Dreams, for that's what I intend. Fund-raising itself is the means, to the end, rather than the end itself. I don't think your job as a fund-raiser is to raise money. It is to fulfill the needs which exist in society, and fund-raising is the way you do that.

I want to thank the people who helped me with this book—The Reverend Robert L. Shearer, Dr. Kenneth H. Crooks, James D. Van Tassel, Harry A. Campbell, Dr. Martin Tangora, and Arnold Leland. Also, my thanks to my many clients and students from whom I've gotten a tremendous education. My special thanks to Daniel R. Harding, of the Center for Direct Marketing. Without him, this book wouldn't have been possible.

In the rush of getting the book done, I am indebted to my assistant, Sandra C. MacDonald and to Jeffrey W. Dawson. Their many suggestions improved the book tremendously.

D.L.C.

Techniques of fund-raising

1 Where is the fun in fund-raising?

As you know, when Columbus set sail to find a new route to the East, everyone thought he would fail because, of course, the world was flat.

They thought there was only one way to reach the East: overland. And only very hearty men could do it, because the route was very dangerous.

Many fund-raisers take a similar one-method approach toward soliciting gifts, and it too is the result of wrong view of the world. This approach involves telling the prospective donor about the administrative side of the organization. Telling him about the budget needs of the organization, the equipment needs, and about its need for new buildings or additions to present buildings. The donor is supposed to respond by giving to the "needs."

The main reason for all this talk about administrative needs is that charities feel that if they didn't emphasize these "concrete" elements, they wouldn't be giving anything back to the donor in exchange for his money. They are, of course, assuming when they do this, that they have nothing else to offer. But this is wrong.

By understanding the function of the charity in the world, the emphasis on administrative needs can be ended. Then you can be free to emphasize the things that really matter to donors, and your reward will be an easier time of raising money and faster growth for your organization.

So, the whole point of this is to give you a real sense of the values you give the donor when he contributes. My goal is to make you realize the giving situation is one in which both you and the donor "win." You do not win at the expense of the donor, nor does the donor win at your expense.

To get this real sense of value, we'll go into three areas:

1. *Necklace Theory*. This is a diagram that explains the relationship between the charity and its function in the world on one hand, and the relationship between the charity and the donor on the other.

2. *The Roles Charities Play*. Because most charities don't understand their function in the world, they play a lot of roles that do more harm than good. We'll look at the bad roles to decide where the mistakes are, then decide on what basis to act in better roles.

3. *Transaction Analysis*. This is basically a look into the values that are being exchanged between the donor and the charity when a donation is made. This will help us decide what to emphasize when we talk to a potential donor, because we'll have some idea not only of what he wants, but also of what we have to offer.

Necklace theory

Probably the most important area is the first, the Necklace Theory. It is a picture of the world shared by most charities today. You can remember it by thinking of a necklace, unclasped, lying on a table, viewed from above. This diagram represents the "world-view" you'd see. (See Figure 1.)

The entire point of the Necklace Theory is that Donor Needs should be matched up to the Needs of Society, and your strongest fund-raising appeal is here. The most important part of the necklace is not the bauble in the middle (the organization) but rather, the clasp between the two ends. This is what gives the whole necklace a purpose, a meaningful function. The proper role of the organization is to put together Donor Needs and the Needs of Society, with itself acting as a means (conduit) to that end. When the organization acts in the capacity, it gives maximum validity to its existence.

In the middle of the diagram (necklace) is the organization as the focal point, the pendant. In this case, "organization" means specifically the bricks and mortar, administrative staff, and equipment.

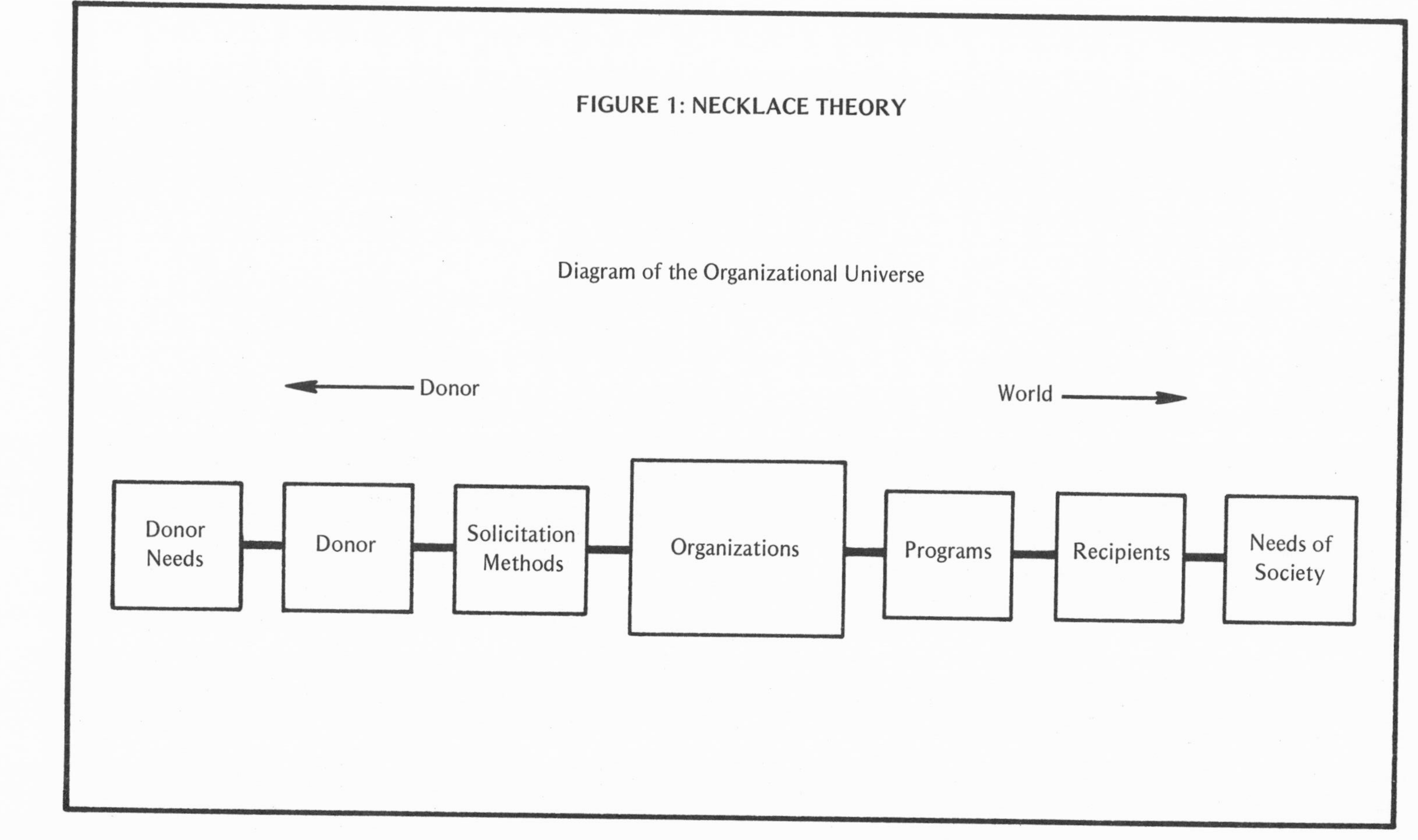
FIGURE 1: NECKLACE THEORY
Diagram of the Organizational Universe
Donor
World
Donor Needs
Donor
Solicitation Methods
Organizations
Programs
Recipients
Needs of Society

I am amazed at how many charities try to raise money based on the needs in this area. In a sense, this is certainly understandable, however, because when non-profit organizations have problems, it is usually in the area of physical facilities or staff or equipment. Many board members, volunteers and even staff think, as a result of "feeling the pinch" in these areas, that they should be the basis of the fund-raising appeal. They take this psychological position: "Mr. Donor, wouldn't you like to help us to remove our pinch?" And it is staggering that donors contribute on this basis!

A similar view is put forth in 80 to 90 per cent of all fund-raising brochures produced today. Take the case of hospitals that want to add a new wing to increase capacity. Invariably, it then creates a brochure which discusses the new wing in much detail. There are schematic drawings, rooms labeled individually, huge lists of equipment (whose functions are unknown, perhaps even unknowable), followed by cost figures for that equipment which would stagger the average donor, and much talk about the cost of the whole project.

Almost nowhere can you find a person in this mass of detail. Unless it's the General Chairman of the Campaign telling you to *give*. In these fund-raising brochures, the prospective donor becomes almost a means to an end: he is valuable only because he gives his money for the greater good—namely, the new hospital wing.

You would think from looking at these brochures that hospitals served no useful, meaningful purpose in the world. Frequently, it's never mentioned that more lives will be saved by building the new wing. Seldom is it mentioned that the prospective donor may himself (in the future) benefit from a donation to this worthy cause.

In other words, the hospital brochure-makers have not painted a picture that explained clearly the role of the hospital wing in the life of the community. And they have forgotten to tell the donor how he fits into this picture, what his function is in this project.

This kind of thinking is very dangerous. It emphasizes exactly the wrong things in a fund-raising appeal, and you could say this kind of thinking totally avoids any fund-raising appeal. It is amazing that millions of dollars are raised every year by institutions which follow this kind of logic. In many cases, it strikes me that donors and fund-raisers have an agreement not to mention the reason for the hospital wing. In a sense, donors end up giving not *because* of the charity, but in spite of it.

So, it is possible to raise money by concentrating on this point (the pendant) in the diagram, but, in so doing, it perpetuates a sickness which should not exist. Money should not be raised for buildings, bricks and mortar. Money should be raised to meet certain needs which exist in society. Buildings, bricks and mortar are only the means for achieving the end of fulfilling the needs which exist in society. In other words, fund-raisers suffer from not having a clear idea of exactly why they are raising this money.

Look at the Necklace diagram again, this time moving one step to the right of the organization (the pendant) is the link "Programs." The Programs are the activities which are carried on by the organization, in the buildings, with the equipment, and with the administrative staff. Also included in Programs are the "faculty" or people who are directly involved with the execution of the various programs. They are separate and distinct from the administrative staff (overhead) I mentioned before.

Some organizations, especially those without fine new buildings, fancy equipment and large administrative staffs, emphasize their programs as their chief "selling point." Really, these organizations feel that they should talk about buildings, staff, and equipment (in part because most other organizations do), but since they may not have reached that stage in their development, they can't. So they talk about their programs: what they are, who they serve, how much it costs to serve them, etc. These organizations make the same mistake as the ones who concentrate on bricks and mortar.

The next step to the right in the Necklace Theory diagram is "Recipients." The Recipients participate in the programs held in the Organization's facilities.

Many newly-formed organizations exist and raise money on the basis of the recipients. In older institutions, the recipients are, or tend to be, neglected in favor of "Programs" and the "Organization" itself. If you are going to make a mistake in emphasis, however, this is certainly the most acceptable area. When in doubt, illustrate your brochures and other publications with many pictures which tell the "situation" of your recipients.

The true emphasis of any organization is concentration on the needs which exist in society. This is why any organization exists, even profit-making ones. "Find a need and fill it" should be the motto of non-profit organizations, too. For most charities, it is only necessary to figure out what needs they are already fulfilling, rather than trying to figure out what needs should be fulfilled. In this thinking process, it is necessary to get down to the most basic reduction possible. The hospital is solving society's need to have health care and to save people's lives. The university is fulfilling society's need for educated citizens.

The needs of society are the strongest possible base on which to rest the appeal of an organization. This is the purpose for which it exists and it should always be mentioned in letters, publicity and public relations materials. It should also be talked about frequently to the membership, volunteers, staff and recipients themselves. It is to fulfill these needs that donors will give the largest amounts of money, easily, for the longest amount of time.

Two organizations that do this well (emphasize the needs of society) are Save the Children Federation and Christian Children's Fund. When you see one of their ads or receive one of their mailing pieces, you are immediately hit with the needs which must be fulfilled. And it is a very compelling and involving image that brings in many contributions.

The next link in the diagram is Solicitation Methods, which are the ways the gifts are gotten. This is the true area of technique in fund-raising. Different solicitation strategies (i.e., whether to use direct mail or personal approach on specific group of prospects) are part of this area. Organizations that emphasize this area tend to place a lot of faith in statistical averages to raise money for them. If they call on enough people, or send enough mailers, they will get a certain number of responses. This is a numbers game and does not bear much resemblance to the real reason for the organizations' existence.

The next link in the diagram is the Donor himself. Organizations that emphasize this area typically have large research departments and feel it is unwise to call on a donor without knowing as much as possible about him. Organizations with the strongest types of appeals (universities, hospitals, cultural organizations, and churches), typically have large research departments (if they have one at all).

But the level you should try to reach is one step beyond the Donor. It is the Donor's Needs. Other terms for it are Donor Values and Donor Self-Image.

If you were to ask a donor to define himself, he might begin to tell you a number of things about himself. He might say he thought of himself as a religious person, an American, a believer in democracy, a liberal. In other words, a man might define himself by telling you what he believes. It is this belief structure which comprises Donor Values and Donor

Needs. The donor's Self-Image is the sum-total of these needs and values.

It is obvious that a person must do more than just think about a certain set of values in order to truly believe them. He must back his words with actions or face being a hypocrite. In other words, he can't just say he is a religious person without doing something religious (i.e., going to church, contributing to church, reading the Bible, volunteering to teach Sunday School, praying, etc.).

Here is where you can help fulfill the needs of your donors. But donors want a lot for their money. Take the example of Mr. Parsimonious who goes to church an hour a week, fifty weeks a year (two weeks for vacation). Fifty hours a year is .57 per cent of the total amount of hours available to him. In addition, he contributes $1.00 a week, forty-eight weeks a year, and $5.00 each on Christmas and Easter (a total of $58.00) which, if he has an annual income of $10,000., is .58 per cent of his income. So, for a total investment of 1.15 per cent of his total available assets of time and money, he may receive as much as 25 per cent of his total self-image. He is not being a hypocrite. He can truly say (to himself, if not to others) that he is a religious person. And this is a true and accurate statement of the facts because he is justified in regarding himself as a religious person. He has done more than just think about religion. He has backed up his beliefs with actions and money.

Please note that, for very little investment on his part, 1.15 per cent of his total available time and money, he has gotten back an enormous amount of self-image. This is not at all unusual; it is the rule rather than the exception. Donors frequently want an enormous return on their investment. Rather than fight this urge on the part of the donors, you should try to portray this return to the greatest possible extent.

Roles characters play

When you take the wrong view of your function to the donor and society, fund-raising becomes an objectionable and distasteful task. Then you begin to act out several unpleasant roles:

1. Beggar
2. Bill Collector
3. Salesman
4. The Artful Dodger
5. Panderer

These five roles that charities play fall into two broad categories: (1) Master and (2) Servant. These two elements may seem as different as night and day, but they spring from the same fallacy: not fully understanding the benefits they give back to the donor. As a result, they feel either superior to the donor (and exploit him) or they feel lower (lowly) and act subservient to him.

The Beggar is the worst role you can possibly play, and it's probably the easiest for you to fall into, as well as the most common. What is wrong with the role of beggar? Basically, you are asking without giving anything in return. When you play this role, you feel guilty because you are simply asking for money for yourself. You do this by asking for their budgets, for staff, for buildings, for programs, etc. You aren't asking that certain needs in society be met, only that money be given. The role of guilt in fund-raising is substantial, especially when charities act like beggars. It is no wonder at such times that volunteers (and even staff) do not wish to engage in fund-raising. Fund-raising in this role becomes the end in itself rather than the means to the greater end. Raising money itself is at most a boring task that is only faintly interesting to those who wish to do combat in the field with certain prospective donors. But when raising money is seen as a means to an end (when the needs in society are being fulfilled, and the donors are being given the opportunity to fulfill their self-images), fund-raising becomes a fascinating and interesting way of living in the world.

The second role, that of Bill Collector, is also very common. Here you say to your donors, "Well, it's that time of year for you to contribute again." The most compelling reason you can find to tell the potential donor that he should give is the time of year. You are not interested in the customer (donor) and whether his needs have been satisfied. You are just interested in seeing the bill paid.

When you act as a Salesman, the third role, a basic conflict appears in the mind of the prospective donor. He is not sure whether you are trying to satisfy your needs or his needs; whether the salesman is trying to sell him a product he doesn't need just for the commissions it will produce. The best salesmen, of course, try to make you feel that they are sincerely interested in meeting your needs, but usually this happens only after a feeling of mutual trust is established. And normally this takes a lot of time.

If you take this position, prospective donors feel that they are valued mostly for their money, not for themselves or their thoughts. Donors will give if they are "sold a bill of goods," but they will be left with a bad taste in their mouth. They will not be interested in continuing their giving, let alone increase their gifts.

The Artful Doger is the position of the charity that pursues the role of Salesman to its logical extremes. In this role, the charity assumes that donors are there expressly for the purpose of providing for the continuation of the charity itself (or its good works). Donors are told that it is their duty to give and are told they should feel guilty if they do not contribute. Some religious and quasi-religious charities fall into this category. The Artful Dodger is there to "pick their pockets."

The fifth role is that of the Panderer. The Panderer caters to or profits from the weaknesses or vices of others, and this role is frequently found among the sympathy charities. It is a basic disregard of the donor as a person with thoughts and feeling; a viewing of him more as an object to be used for certain ends. This is sometimes found among charities which protect animals, save children and educate the "heathens." Surprisingly, it is also found in some elements of certain political movements (McCarthyism, for example).

What should charities be? There are five roles that are positive and beneficial to both the donor and charity. They are:

1. Broker
2. Wholesaler/Subdivider
3. Executor
4. Evangelist
5. Tom Sawyer

A Broker puts buyer's needs and seller's needs together (earning a commission for his matchmaking. The best example of this is a real estate broker who is only happy when both the buyer and the seller are happy with the transaction. In other words, the transaction is best where everybody wins and nobody loses. In game theory, this is called the zero sum game. (Everyone ends the game with no score.)

You should play the role of broker between the donor on one hand and society (the needs of society) on the other. It is your function to point out to the donor (and sometimes to society) that this is a game in which everybody wins. As in the case of true brokers, charities who play this role collect a fee for their services. Donors who object to this fee are irrational. The only philosophical choice a donor has is whether to have the needs of society fulfilled or not. There is no other possible choice. To have the government fill the role of private philanthropy is just to abdicate control over the situation. The broker's fee will be taken out of the funds by the government.

The charity should also act in the role of Wholesaler/Subdivider of "good works." In contrast to the role of Wholesaler, many charities act as Retailers with a hefty mark-up. They reveal this when they talk about the increase in operating costs this year and the small amount of money scheduled (budgeted) to come in. Such charities seem to be flaunting their inefficiency of management in front of prospective donors and seem to be taunting the donor to throw his money in a sewer.

Donors do not want to know how their money is being spent. They want to know how their needs are being met and how the needs of society are being met. And while they are not interested in the gory details of the budget and administrative staff changes, etc., they *are* interested in knowing that their money is being administered efficiently and effectively. Charities that plead poverty do not instill confidence in their donors. Wholesalers of good works make it very clear to the donor that his $5.00 or $10.00 this year will help one more boy get a decent start in life, or will help feed thirty refugees for a week, or achieve similar results. Whole salers allow you to participate in good works without your having to give up substantial amounts of time and money, and, as such, they provide a valuable function in society.

Subdividers are very similar to Wholesalers. A Subdivider in real estate buys large portions of land (say 1,000 to 10,000 acres) and divides it into smaller, more easily purchased pracels (say ¼ acre). Very few people could afford to buy the large portion of land, but many people can afford the smaller parcels.

Many charities do not realize they are providing a similar service for their donors. Most people could never afford to do good works on the scale that charities work. If a man wanted to start a hospital in Africa, let's say, he would have to give up his present life-style, his career, move to Africa, spend thousands of dollars, and spent most of his life trying to build this project. It's possible for the same man not to give up any of those things and still accomplish the same end. All he has to do is find the non-profit organization that will do it for him. He may then sit in the comfort of his home, carry on his regular life, and still feel as though he has a part of these good works. Charities subdivide good works and "sell" them in manageable proportions to others who could not buy them if they had to do it themselves. You should not fail to point out this function you are filling to your donors.

The role of Executor is talking about what an efficient administrator you are. The donor should be convinced that his money is being spent better in Charity A than Charity B. In the strictest sense, an executor is one who administers an estate on behalf of another (in this case, the estate of the donor is being administered by the charity). It's your duty, as a charity, to loudly and constantly tell the donors you are a competent and efficient administrator of their funds.

An Evangelist has an inner strength which enables him to enlist others to his point of view. It's unfortunate that the image of the Evangelist has been tarnished by movies that portray him as a huckster or a charlatan, because the role itself is very important. In its original meaning, the word evangel means "good news" and an evangelist is the "bringer of good news." What a marvelous way of looking at the process of persuading others to get involved in your "mission." The Evangelist is not doing something *to* other people. He is letting them in on the good news. He is doing something *for* them. You should think of your fund-raising activities as opportunities for donors to participate in good and worthwhile activities. And you should do all this with a certain amount of religious fervor.

Tom Sawyer was a very clever fellow. Remember how he persuaded his friends to whitewash the fence for him? He made this otherwise tiresome task seem so attractive and so enticing that his friends were willing to pay him for the opportunity to do it. This ability to make common tasks attractive is an art which must be cultivated by you. Volunteers can't be effective in asking for gifts if they don't think the common task of soliciting has a greater purpose or greater meaning.

Transaction analysis

When a gift is made by the donor to the charity, there is a transaction. What are the basic values which are being exchanged in these transactions? See page 28 for the basic value exchange situations.

Whenever someone becomes a beneficiary of an organization's work, he may feel that he has obtained something of continuing value for which

Basic Values	Donor Life Curve[1]	Characteristics
1. Beneficiary Payment	A	long donor life; high average donation; strongest value exchange situation
2. Philosophical Activation	B	medium donor life; medium average donation; moderate value exchange situation
3. Emotional Activation	K	shortest donor life; lowest average donation; temporary (short-lived) value exchange situation
4. Recognition Purchase		auxiliary value exchange situation (can be added most successfully to Types 1 & 3 above)
5. Product Purchase		auxiliary value exchange situation (can be added to any of the above types)

[1] See Chapter 6, "How Much Will This Cost You?"

he has continuing debt. These feelings of gratitude and/or obligation are likely to motivate "repayment" donations in the future. A fund-raiser will almost always find it worthwhile to compile and maintain the names of beneficiaries (or "constituents") and to solicit them for a number of years, if necessary, until they finally become donors. This is the only frequently encountered situation where compilation of non-donor names proves justified.

Examples are:

1. Colleges and their alumni
2. Hospitals and their patients
3. Symphony orchestras and their attenders
4. The Red Cross and its disaster aid recipients
5. The YMCA and its members
6. The Heart Fund and survivors of heart disease victims (Sometimes they are not direct "beneficiaries" but they behave similarly because they can appreciate the possibility that they might have been or they wish they could have been.)

You should be aware that solicitations to beneficiaries will only be successful if they feel that supporting the continuing work of the organization also provides satisfaction of *present* emotional and/or philosophical needs.

Philosophical activations are the most common value exchange situation. They are "belief activations," which give the donor the feeling that he is doing more than just paying lip service to ideas which he believes in. Since a person does not easily give up or even change his "philosophy," he tends to stay with the organization for some time and give on a fairly regular basis.

Examples are:

1.	ACLU NAACP Common Cause	Members concerned about political rights and freedoms
2.	Synanon Florence Crittenden Alcoholics Anonymous	Members concerned about rehabilitation of "sick" people
3.	Planned Parenthood Zero Population Growth Sierra Club	Members concerned about over-population and environmental control

Emotional Activations are a factor in most donation transactions. The donor's "revenue" is the satisfaction obtained from being able to activate emotions which previously had no outlet. Some common emotional activations are: fear, love, and anger.

Recognition Purchases are most commonly used with donors to cultural organizations and hospitals. Certain social status benefits are involved. Recognition usually involves listing donor names in a publication or on a plaque. One obstacle to the broader use of this incentive is the fact that it tends to lose impact when large numbers of donor names are involved.

Product Purchases are sometimes referred to as "fulfillment offers." In this case, a product for which there is genuine consumer demand is offered as a stimulus to the basic emotional or philosophical activation.

Examples of fulfillment offers are:

1. Museum memberships
2. Symphony and opera subscriptions
3. UNICEF Christmas cards
4. Olympic team donor shoulder patches
5. College alumni magazines
6. Sierra Club books

2 Stalking the big gift

Of all the ways to raise money, a major gift program is probably the easiest. Not that raising large sums from a few wealthy individuals is an easy task, but the resources required by the organization are few, and under most circumstances, available.

What are these readily available components? Basically, they are:

1. Someone who is involved in, committed to, and cares about the needs which exist in society (for which the organization was formed)
2. Someone dedicated enough to fulfilling the needs that exist in society to spend time doing research (in the library and with the donor himself)
3. Prospective donors who feel the same way about fulfilling the needs in society
4. Time and place
5. Verbal or written proposal

What could be simpler? Just two people representing the organization, a proposal, a time, a place, and several prospects (seen only one at a time, of course). These are the elements in any major gift solicitation, no matter what the size of your organization. But how do you put these elements together to get the gift?

What strategy should be used? Basically, it is that the fund-raising project should be designed for the donor. Above all, it should meet his needs, fulfill his value-structure. This means that you should not develop the fund-raising project before you have the donor-prospect in mind. Or to put it another way, you should not set a fund-raising goal and then go look for prospects. First you must find the prospects. Then design a fund-raising "product" which they will be interested in donating to and then present it to them.

In the business world, this is known as the marketing approach. First, the advertising is developed and tested; then, if enough orders are received for the product, the product is made.

The Point: You should

1. Find out what you're all about; where you are going.
2. Find a person who has money and a problem.
3. Tell that person how you can solve his problem.

What are the practical implications of this point of view? Let's look at a hypothetical example.

SAN FRANCISCO (AP)— Dan Angelo, prominent San Franciscan, today announced the sale of his Angelo Travel Agency to Diners Club. The Angelo Travel Agency has ninety-four offices world-wide, located in eighty-two countries.

Mr. Angelo, said the sale was forced because of his health. He is known to have a heart condition. He will retire when the sale is completed.

Mr. Angelo began his travel agency business over forty years ago in a small one-man office here. Since that time, his business has grown very rapidly, and Mr. Angelo has boasted to several friends that "I've never had an unprofitable year."

Mr. Angelo came to San Francisco from Italy fifty-two years ago. One of the first organizations he joined was the Boy Scouts, Troup 114. He has been active in many San Francisco organizations since then, including the de Young Museum, the San Francisco Symphony, the San Francisco Opera and the San Francisco Ballet. He has also been active abroad, especially with the Save Venice Foundation.

Mr. Angelo has brought an Eastern influence to many of the cultural organizations he belongs to after he converted from Catholicism to Buddhism thirteen years ago. Also, Mr. Angelo was instrumental in getting the National Headquarters of the Buddhist Church of America moved to San Francisco.

Mrs. Angelo's wife, Philomena, died two years ago of cancer. His daughter, Mrs. James Rockefeller of New York City, is his only living relative. Mrs. Rockefeller, three years ago, was convicted of possession of marijuana, but was given a suspended sentence.

It is obvious that Mr. Angelo, no matter what else he is, is a good prospect for a major gift. Why is this so? First of all, we know that he is predisposed to giving to charities. He's got the habit. It is also clear that many projects could be created to appeal to his interests. The task is to convince him that your project is the best way for him to fulfill his interests.

What are the ways to solicit him? Here are thirty-nine projects he might be interested in:

1. Boy Scouts of America: "Mr. Angelo, did you learn anything as a Boy Scout that helped you to become successful in your business? Here is a project which will help to carry on those same ideals?"
2. Japanese-American Community Center: (a) Buddhist temple in the center (b) Cultural wing (c) Youth wing (d) Old people's health wing.
3. Set up a foundation; put all his money into it; dispense according to his interests.
4. Italian-American committee: develop traveling exhibit of major Italian art.
5. Heart association: research on heart disease
6. Catholic church retreat center
7. Buddhist meditation center
8. Cultural exchange program for students
9. Cancer Society: program for people who recover
10. Cancer Society: program for early warning detection of cancer
11. Youth center
12. Drug rehabilitation center
13. Asian studies program in universities
14. Cultural program for youth groups
15. Travel society for the elderly
16. Asian art wing on museum
17. Italian art wing on art museum
18. Boys' Club (boys' home) for Italian-Americans
19. Girls' Club (girls' home) for Italian-Americans
20. Home for minority group children
21. Children's music center
22. Medical program for the elderly poor

23. Scholarships for students who want to learn about small business
24. Sponsor a tour of an Asian ballet company
25. Underwrite new production of Puccini's *Madama Butterfly*
26. Commission a new symphony
27. Bring an Asian conductor to San Francisco Symphony
28. Sponsor Japanese No play at American Conservatory Theater
29. Neighborhood Arts Center—sponsor program
30. World Friendship Organization
31. International Visitors Association
32. San Francisco Chamber of Commerce/businessman's exchange program
33. Restore early Italianate architecture in Northern California
34. Businessman's Association for Cultural Betterment of the City of San Francisco—start a new organization
35. New hospital wing—cardiac care
36. New hospital wing—cancer treatment
37. Senior citizen's center
38. New cultural center for San Francisco
39. Italian-American anti-defamation league

What are all these "ways" to solicit Dan Angelo? They are nothing more than designing a project or service to meet his needs, his interests, his value-structure. And I hope it's obvious that this list could be extended almost forever.

Don't let the point escape you. These projects do not start with the charity as a point of reference. They start with Dan Angelo and his interests. Most charities do not do this. They are hidebound and restricted by what they think are the restrictions placed on them by the needs of their organization. Many solicitations fail, in my opinion, because you can't rid yourself of this point of view. It's really a kind of paralysis that must be wiped out if you intend to maximize your fund-raising efforts.

But, you say, this sounds all very simple if you happen to be a charity that is one of Dan Angelo's interests. But what if you're not?

Let's approach this problem gradually.

1. For the moment, think of yourself as a charity that Dan Angelo has given to. Your job seems simple enough. But how would you approach him? What strategy would you use? Would you try to appeal to

even more of his interests? This would probably be the most successful.

2. Now think of yourself as a charity that works in a wider, related area of Dan Angelo's interest. For example, the arts, travel, business, youth, health, old age. How would you approach him? What strategy would you use?

3. Last, think of yourself as a charity unrelated to Dan Angelo's known interests. For example, a liberal or a conservative political cause, population control, environmental protection, Judaism, a Chicago student scholarship program. How would you approach him? What strategy would you use?

The principle is the same in all three cases: Appeal to Dan Angelo's interests. The most difficult one is the third. This is really the same problem as the charity with a small group of potential members. How do they raise larger amounts of money than the limits of their members? In a sense, the answer is quite simple: get more members. This means that you must expand your charity beyond its present boundaries. Expand its purpose. Become what you are not now. Start a project or set up a "subsidiary" that has a wider possible membership (appeal). In other words, find an area of agreement and talk about that. If you don't have one, go create one.

Let's look at three possible ways to approach Dan Angelo if you were a charity basically unrelated to his interests. In the case of a minority program: Mr. Angelo is a member of a minority group. Do you think he would feel that other minority groups should also be helped? Or does he discriminate between minority groups?

In the case of population control and environmental protection: "Mr. Angelo, do you think the world was better thirty years ago or today?"

In the case of the political cause: "Mr. Angelo, how do you feel about government regulation of small business?"

If you can get him involved at this point, you can at least get him to seriously consider making a gift to an organization he may never even have heard of before. If you cannot get him involved at this point, do not pursue the discussion any further. If you cannot find a common ground right away, and get him in the habit of saying "yes," you will probably fail. Leave him and go on to the next prospect.

But, you say, does this mean that charities should be like chameleons, changing today to fit one donor, tomorrow to fit another? Should a charity try to be all things to all people?

Yes. At least you should try. By all means try. There are limits to your changeability, but you'd probably be startled to find out how flexible you really are. The advantage of trying to be changeable is that you will be more successful more of the time. "Success" not only means raising more money, but also doing a better job of providing the service of your charity. My theory here is that the best service of any charity is one that fits the needs of the donors. The needs of the donors reflect the needs of society, and if you fulfill one, you fulfill the other.

Here is a list of some possible "subsidiaries" or projects almost any church could start. These are in addition to its religious or spiritual function.

1. Home for the aged
2. Hospital
3. Senior center
4. Youth center
5. Home for unwed mothers
6. Seminary
7. College
8. High school
9. Elementary school
10. Day care center
11. Drug clinic
12. Drop-in center
13. Information switchboard
14. Newspaper
15. Radio station
16. TV station
17. Sanitarium
18. Orphanage
19. Counseling program
20. Subsidized housing program for minorities
21. Missions
22. Missionaries
23. Feeding the poor
24. Seminars
25. Lectures
26. Magazines

27. Minority group development program
28. Camps
29. Retreats
30. Nurse training
31. Teacher training
32. Farms
33. Manufacturing firms
34. Organizational development consulting
35. Family planning clinics
36. Publishing firms
37. Greeting cards
38. Religious items
39. Tract publishing
40. Used furniture and clothing store
41. Apartment house
42. Real estate development
43. Retirement villages

This list means only one thing to me. A church can be many things other than a church. There is almost nothing it can't do! (At least theoretically.)

What are the practical limits on future development? What you will become depends on:

1. What you're interested in.
2. What your resources are (time and money).

You ought to have a list similar to the one above which lists all the things you'd like to be if you had the time and the money. Keep that list in readiness. You never know when you'll run across another Dan Angelo in the evening paper.

Another thing to be learned from this list is that you must be flexible at presentations. When you do not know the prospect especially well, you should be able to go from one project to another (because you know the Master Plan) with ease. The essence of getting the gift by this method is a lot of advance planning and an ability to be flexible at the presentation.

I think you could even be totally unrelated to any of his known interests and still stand a very good chance of getting a gift. For example, you could be a small, coeducational college in the Eastern United States he has never heard of. But you might be able to get a donation by offering him a type of deferred giving program (a non-revokable life income trust) which would reduce his taxes dramatically and at the same time give him a secure income for life. Nothing to do with the cause or a project, but it meets his needs; follows his interests.

When you go to see a prospect, you should ask yourself these questions: What sort of a person does this man think he is and what would he like to be? What kind of a man does he believe other people think he is? What would he like to have others think about him? These are obviously not very "hard" questions you could get very definite answers to. But this is to get you to focus your attention on the prospect and his hopes, his needs, and his aims in life. Sometimes the job is even more difficult because you must help the prospect form a self-concept that was vauge or even unformed.

You should be aware that most of the big gift money raised in the United States today is not raised in this manner. So this change in emphasis to the prospect is not a guaranteed method of being 100 per cent successful, but it will be more successful than playing a numbers game.

When face to face with the prospect, you should ask as many involving questions as possible. Such questions are: How may I help you? How can I be of service to you? What are you interested in? What problems do you have? What do you believe in? Can we find an area of common ground? Can we find an area of common agreement?

Don't forget the main point: Design the project to fit the donor's needs.

How to raise $1,000,000 when you have no money, no organization, no program and no members

This may sound unreal, but it's quite common in the business world. All you really need is well thought-out plans to get that kind of money. Let's look at a real estate developer who discovers some farm acreage not too far from town.

1. He does some research on population movement in the area.
2. He buys an option on the farm acreage.
3. He hires an architect.

4. The architect draws up plans for an apartment house complex.
5. The developer takes his research and his plans to a bank (or other lenders).
6. He receives $3.6 million to build the apartment house complex. Lenders will give money on well-thought-out plans that help them make more money. After all, they're in the business of making loans ("renting" out their money). They will gladly give money for good plans.

Use the same process with big gift prospects. Find a rich prospect. Find out what his needs and interests are, then approach him with a well thought-out project which meets his needs. You should view your project as an "opportunity" for the prospect to fulfill his needs, to pursue his interests.

What is the best time to solicit a major gift?

Various experiences and events occur in a person's life which make him more likely to give a larger donation than he would ordinarily make. When those experiences or events occur, he enters an important Time Window known as "hunting season."

But what happens before and after "hunting season"? Then you will receive an "ordinary" gift. The amount will be the usual sum he would give to anyone who had a reasonable cause. He gives this amount to them because of the "nuisance value" of the request, as much as any other reason. He's not very interested in charity to get really involved, really committed. Also, his needs are not very great at this time.

But in "hunting season" you are capable of getting a larger gift. His needs and interests have increased. What are the Time Window characteristics for Dan Angelo?

1. *Money*. The simple fact that he is selling his business means he has more money and is capable of giving more.

2. *Health*. Because his health is failing, he would naturally begin to be more concerned about this than in the past. His wife's death from cancer contributes to this. You could guess that he's becoming more aware of his own life coming to an end.

3. *Age.* He is becoming wiser (?) more introspective (?) looking to perpetuate his beliefs (?) looking for immortality (?).

4. *Retirement.* Civic-minded already, now has much free time to pursue his interests. "Do you have any dreams you'd like to see fulfilled, Mr. Angelo?"

5. *Wife's death.* When is the proper time to solicit the survivor after the spouse's death? Many cautious fund-raisers say between eighteen and twenty-four months. Others say six to twelve months. The boundaries are set in both cases by two considerations. If the solicitation is too soon after the death, discussing the deceased spouse may be too painful. On the other hand, if it's too long after the death, the surviving spouse may remarry. Whatever boundaries you decide, look up the obituary columns from your local newspaper during that period. They are an excellent source of surviving spouses.

6. *Daughter's marijuana conviction.* Makes him more likely, even though he's old, to give to youth or drug programs. There are boundary questions here, too. Too soon, it may be too painful. Too late, he may have forgotten about it. Look in the public court records for convictions and suspended sentences of youths, eighteen to twenty-four months ago. Then go see the parents about starting a drug prevention program.

All of these six Time Windows have a definite beginning and a definite ending. If you were to graph the first example, money, you would get this:

How long is this Time Window? If this were June 29, he would have exactly six months and one day to decide what to do with the money. By December 31 he must make up his mind or he will loose a substantial amount to the Internal Revenue Service.

Before he enters the Time Window, he gives an ordinary gift. This will vary from person to person. Let's assume Dan Angelo will give $100 as his ordinary gift. When he enters the Time Window, he becomes a candidate for giving $1,000,000-plus. The reason for the plus is that we know that he has more money than that, but we don't know exactly how much. Over the course of the Time Window, Mr. Angelo begins to back down to his former level of "ordinary" giving. Over time, he begins to commit his money to different projects (investments).

Let's look at some other Time Windows you may find in other prospects.

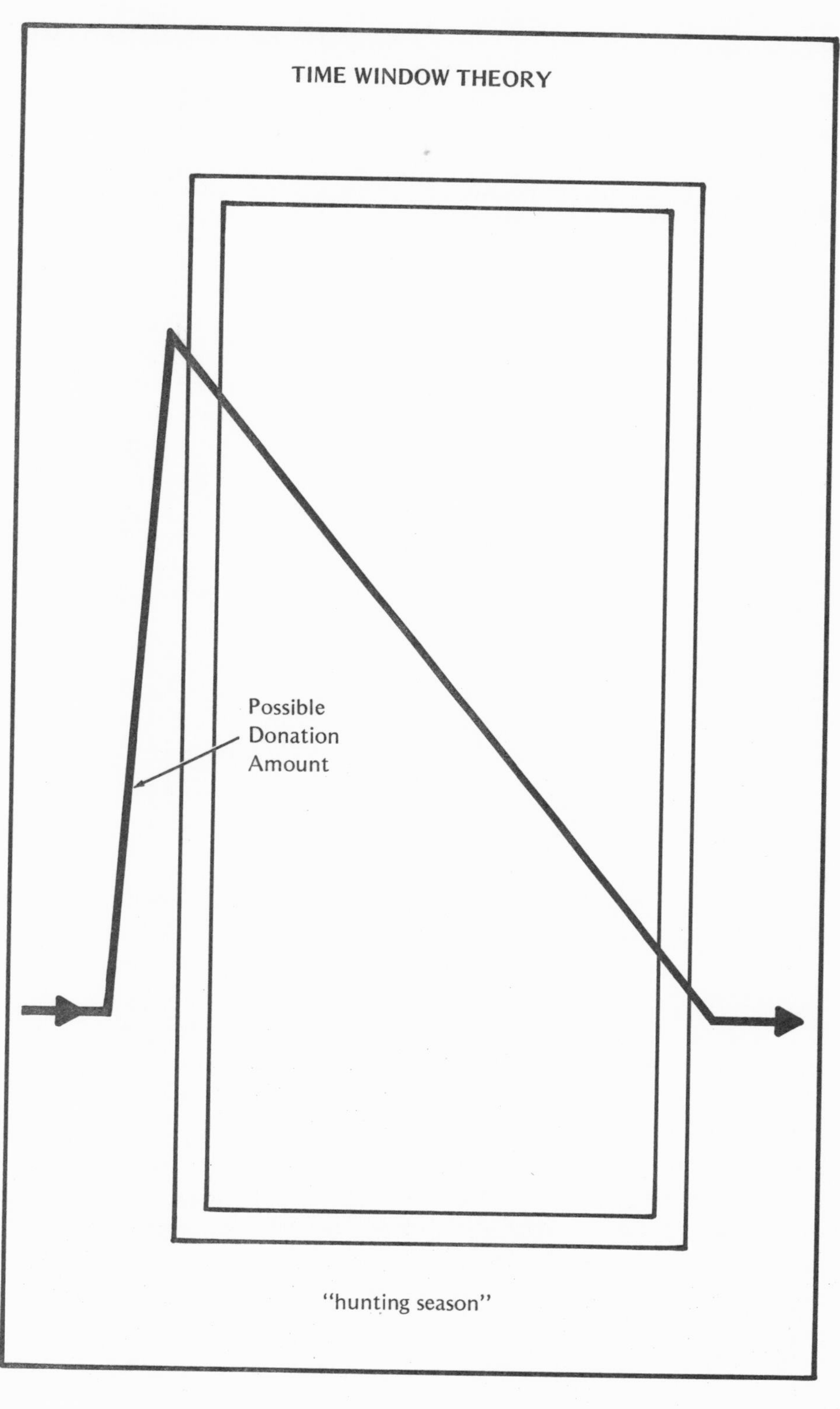
TIME WINDOW THEORY
Possible
Donation
Amount
"hunting season"

Eleven time windows to look for

1. *Cash (new money).* People who have new money rather than old money are better prospects because they usually haven't thought about how to spend it and also they feel guilty about having so much. Old money usually knows exactly what to do with money and they don't feel guilty. There are two major ways to getting new money—inheritance and the sale of an asset. In both cases, there is much publicly available information. Both the probation of wills and the sales of real estate are publicly recorded.

2. *Company goes public.* The magazine *Investment Dealer's Digest* lists all companies that are planning to sell their stock to the public. If you find a company listed here that does business in your town or state, you should write for a prospectus. It will list all the company officers, their home addresses, their salaries, and the number of shares of the company stock they own. Then to make this information even more useful, you should know the companies your members work for. When a company goes public, most of the officers normally become far richer men than they used to be. Then they enter the Time Window!

3. *Company already publicly held* (New York Stock Exchange, American Stock Exchange, regional stock exchanges, over-the-counter markets). Look in the Security and Exchange Commission's *Insider's Report* for a change in any officer or insider's stock holdings in that company. Any change in holdings tells you that his financial position is changing. Perhaps he needs a tax deduction or an estate planning session. He has just entered the Time Window.

4. *Interests elsewhere.* Consequences are that assets are no longer needed. Disinterest may effect such things as a boat, a second car, a vacation home, a camper, a mobile home, anything that may have outlived its usefulness to the prospect. One way to discover this Time Window is to publish in your newsletter that you want such items, and that you stand ready to give a donation receipt for the item's current market value.

Probably the greatest potential in this area is tax shelters. Three major types of tax shelters are oil drilling funds, real estate syndications, and cattle feeding programs. They are investments designed to give the buyer a tax deduction. Over $10 billion of tax shelters have been sold in the last ten years. And buyers must be rich to be able to buy them in most states. In California, buyers must have earned $50,000 per year, or be in the 50 per cent Federal Income Tax bracket, or have a net worth of $100,000.

For you, the interesting feature about tax shelters is that they cannot be sold once they are purchased, but they may be transferred. And when they are transferred to a charity, the donor may deduct the full market value of the gift from his taxes. So the donor gets a double tax deduction —first when he buys the tax shelter, second when he donates it.

You should put a large notice in your newsletter to members stating that you accept donations of tax sheltered investments. You should say also that this and all other gifts made to your charity are fully tax deductible. Many charities don't even know if their members own these kinds of investments and many members don't know they could donate these investments. See your charity's attorney about the legal aspects of receiving them (just as you would check with him about any unusual gift such as real estate or stocks), then start sending out the word. You will be pleasantly surprised at the results.

5. *Extraordinary income.* Stock market profits, real estate profits, salary increases for top executives and executive year-end bonuses are all examples of this area. Certain groups of professionals have large income fluctuations. Some of the people with the greatest fluctuations are: lawyers, dentists, engineers, architects, psychologists, CPAs. In lean years, they're not very good prospects. In fat years, they might seriously be interested in a tax deduction of major size. Find these people by knowing your members who are professionals and send them a series of special mailings alerting them to your availability as a place for them to get a tax deduction when they need it. For professionals who are not your members, you should advertise in their professional publications.

6. *No longer any need to provide an estate.* (Death of spouse.)

7. *Desire to make other investments.* (Yearn for liquidity.) Sometimes it's difficult to sell some assets. But donors can give them to charity and get a tax deduction, thereby freeing money that would otherwise go for taxes to make other investments.

8. *Extraordinary event.* Daughter becomes a drug addict. Cousin gets epilepsy. Relatives enter a Time Window.

9. *Health failing or contemplating death.* Look for older donors—55-plus.

10. *Moves to higher social or business position.* Notices sometimes appear in the local newspaper in the business section. Library has newsletters which have this information. Usually the person in a new social or business position has not yet decided how to spend the increase in money he's going to get, therefore he's a good prospect.

11. *New executive or new professional moves into town.* Newsletters also have this information as well as the local newspaper.

If you follow the Time Window Theory, you will know when to solicit the prospect. If you then design the project to fit the prospect's needs, your chances for getting the gift will increase tremendously. But in a sense, this doesn't tell you very much about the actual face-to-face encounter. How should that work? Here are some simple guidelines.

What to do when you ask for the gift

First, call and:

1. Find out if you have a common interest.
2. Find out what he's interested in.
3. Talk about those aspects of the project he's interested in.
4. Ask him what he thinks of the project.
5. Get him to ask how much money you want.
6. Don't ask for the gift right then. Don't take a pledge card.
7. But ask for another time to see him.

Second, call and:

1. Have answers to questions or objections from first call.
2. Take someone else along? Many times, yes, it increases your chances.
3. Refresh his memory on main points of his interest in the project.
4. Emphasize other pace-setting gifts.
5. Talk memorials again.
6. Get him to talk about points he's interested in in the project.
7. Ask for the gift. Remember—there is no way to get money without asking for it.
8. Leave.

How much should you ask for?

Most people make the mistake of asking for too little. They don't do this because they need less money, but because they think the prospect can't or won't give them more. And this is the result of a guilt-complex they have about their charity and their cause. They feel shy and want to avoid rejection by the prospect.

Rule 1. You'll never get what you ask for.

Rule 2. If you're going to make a mistake, ask for too much rather than too little. It's very difficult to get him to increase his gift, but it's very easy to get him to reduce the amount you ask him for. It's a lot harder to go uphill than down.

So, if the gift he says he'll make is too small, don't accept it right away. Ask if it would be all right to check with your Chairman or Executive Director or President of the Board. In other words, do anything to prolong the negotiations. It is very hard to get him to increase his gift once the card is signed or the letter written.

What you have to offer the prospect

Every charity with tax-exempt organization status has many "products" to offer prospects. So you should view the solicitation of a prospect as an "opportunity" for him to not only fulfill his needs and desires and convictions, but also for him to solve some of his financial problems. All of these matters are aspects of his self-interest.

The message is: You must find a rich prospect and show him how your project can help him with his problems.

These "products" you have to offer can be put into four areas:

1. Tax deduction
2. Liquidity
3. Security and income for life
4. Estate planning aid

These specific "products" are:

1. Memorials
2. Trusts
3. Annuities
4. Tax deduction

5. Life income
6. Liquidity (he can get rid of a "frozen asset")
   a.) Tax shelters (oil drilling funds, cattle feeding program and real estate syndications, etc.)
   b.) Real estate
   c.) Restricted stock
   d.) Art
   e.) Other usually difficult to sell items
7. Bargain sales
8. Reduction of capital gains tax (he can give an appreciated asset).
9. Bequests (you allow the donor to not inconvience his present-day living by giving after death).
10. Life insurance
11. Loan to charity
12. Buy a bond (he can earn 6, 7, 8 per cent, just like a savings account).

After the gift

After the gift, be sure to ask the donor for suggestions of other people who have similar interests. Then ask him to make the calls with you. He should feel good about this if you've done your job. He should feel "relieved and satisfied" that a personal problem has been solved, and he may be interested in helping others feel the same way.

Remember, too, that a present donor is your very best prospect for a future gift. Involve the donor in your charity. Try to get this feeling across: "This organization wants me, wants my ideas and suggestions, as well as my money. They value me as a person."

You should be people-oriented and their problems-oriented. Don't be oriented to simply raising money for a project. Fund-raising is the means to the end, rather than the end itself.

Four tips

1. Keep a "Ten Most Wanted People" file. Review monthly. Ask yourself the question: "How close am I getting to this person?"

2. Make a donor profile. A major health charity in the United States made a study of gifts made through wills. They found:
   a.) The wills were made three to six years prior to receiving the gifts. So the charity did not have to wait a long time.
   b.) Wills were made by a widow or widower.
   c.) Usually there were no heirs or no close heirs.
   d.) Average age at the time the will was made out: 60-62. From this it's obvious that if you could find someone sixty to sixty-two years old, a widow or widower, with no heirs or no close heirs, he would be a great prospect for a gift through a will.
3. Study selling literature. Especially *Successful Low-Pressure Salesmanship* and *Guideposts for Effective Salesmanship*.
4. Get salesmen who are members of your charity to solicit for you; especially stockbrokers, real estate salesmen, and life insurance salesmen.

Where to find rich people

1. Directory of Corporate Affiliation (National Register Publishing Co., Inc.)
2. Dun & Bradstreet's Million Dollar Directory
3. Dun & Bradstreet's Middle Market Directory
4. Fitch Corporation Manuals
5. *Fortune*'s Plant and Product Director
6. MacRae's Blue Book
7. Moody's Industrial Manual (and other manuals).
8. Plan Purchasing Directory
9. Poor's Register of Corporations, Directors and Executives (may be indexed under "Standard & Poor's")
10. Register of Manufacturers for your state or area (e.g., California Manufacturers Register)
11. Standard Register of Advertisers
12. Standard & Poor's Industrial Index
13. Standard & Poor's Listed Stock Reports
14. Thomas' Register of American Manufacturers
15. Walker's Manual of Far Western Corporations and Securities

16. R. L. Polk City Directory
17. Social Register
18. *Who's Who in America* (and other directories)
19. Chamber of Commerce list of members
20. Foundation directory
21. Other organizations' donor lists (that are publicly available)
    a.) Symphony program listings
    b.) Museum membership list
    c.) University alumni magazine
22. Other organizations' board members
23. Membership lists of exclusive social clubs
24. Telephone book yellow pages for:
    a.) Doctors
    b.) Lawyers
    c.) Dentists
    d.) Accountants
    e.) Engineers
    f.) Architects
    g.) Management consultants
    h.) Psychologists
25. Society column in newspaper.
26. Newspaper column of people who are getting a job promotion to top positions in major businesses in your area.
27. "Mailing List" category in telephone book yellow pages.

3 Survival in the direct mail jungle

Direct mail is very weak. Typically, 98 per cent of the people who receive it throw it away. Only 2 per cent respond. And that is success!

Direct mail is weak. You should think of it as "impulse buying" for the people who get it! They will try it if they think it might meet their needs. It is not persuasive to those 98 per cent who do not respond. It is only persuasive to those who are already convinced of the truth of what you're saying. So your job is to find large numbers of people who believe the same things you do. Then send them a direct mail piece that assumes they are already interested in what you have to say to them. Direct mail can only enhance this interest; it can't persuade.

Do not exhort your prospects to share your beliefs, for this is a waste of effort. Assume they share your beliefs already. You should take this approach: "Do you believe that the environment should be protected? Then you should support that belief by sending your check to us today." You should not list all the reasons why you think they should believe the environment should be protected if they don't. If you've ever tried to get someone to change his mind, you know how difficult that can be. People have a perverse way of sticking to their own beliefs even if they are logically shown to be wrong. And that's in person! The bad thing about direct mail is that it can be thrown away the minute the reader disagrees with anything you've said. That's what I mean about its ability to persuade: it doesn't have any. It's too throw-away-able. You will get better results if you spend your time talking to people who already agree with what you have to say.

What are the best ways to persuade? These four are also the ways of selling:

1. Face-to-face
2. Telephone
3. Direct mail
4. Advertising

They are listed in the order of most persuasive to least persuasive. If you're a crusader, don't look to direct mail to do your job for you.

Direct mail is dangerous. I know of no better way for charities to lose a lot of money, if only because there is a lot of money being spent. Direct mail is expensive. If the Little Sisters of the Poor send 10,000 pieces costing 20¢ each, they are spending $2,000. If they get a 2 per cent response rate (200 people) and each sends $5.00, they have income of $1,000. and presto! the Little Sisters of the Poor are poorer by $1,000! That is when you realize that direct mail is dangerous.

It is also objectionable. Twenty-five per cent of the people who get it don't like to get it. And remember, 98 per cent of the people who get it must not like it very much, or they would be responding.

Direct mail is somewhat unpredictable, largely because there are so many possible combinations of parts, size, shape, color, texture, pictures, and words. Each of these seven elements have literally hundreds of possible variations, and that is why even experts can't predict exactly what kind of a response you'll get to a mailing.

If there is one sure rule in direct mail, it is that no direct mail piece will work right all the time. The big element is time. Times change. People think and feel differently about the same issues at different times in their life. And since direct mail is not very persuasive, you must try to figure out if they've changed since the last mailing. And if they have, you must figure out what to say to them so they will continue to give.

Generally, direct mail is only good for getting small gifts ($5.00 to $100.00), and for that to be profitable, you must mail to large numbers of people. And that is very costly and risky. If you try to cut down your costs by mailing to smaller numbers of people, you actually increase the risk! If the Little Sisters of the Poor mail 1,000 pieces instead of 10,000 pieces, their costs are reduced overall, but the cost per piece goes up. As any housewife knows, eggs are cheaper by the dozen than the half-dozen. Let's says that the cost per piece goes up to 25 cents. Total cost is 1,000 × 25 cents or $250.00. However, the response rate remains the same 2 per cent. So twenty people give their $5.00. And presto! the Little Sisters of the Poor just lost $150.00.

But let's have the Little Sisters of the Poor do another mailing, this time to 500,000 people. The cost of each piece drops to 9 cents for a total of $45,000. Again a 2 per cent response or 10,000 gifts. Each gives $5.00 for $50,000 total. So they make $5,000, at last. In direct mail you get small gifts. For it to be profitable, you must mail to large numbers of prospects.

"Well, if direct mail is so bad, why do I get so much of it?" The answer is very simple: It works. Even with all of its risks, it works. Over 50 per cent of the money given to charities last year was raised through direct mail. And that is over $11,000,000,000. Direct mail raises an awful lot of money.

There is only one kind of charity that should not use direct mail: A charity with ten members or less. And even then I would say that it could be used sometimes. But most charities should use direct mail in a big way.

A map, or how do I get out of this place alive?

If you want to stay alive in direct mail, follow these three rules:

1. Save your junk mail
2. Involve the reader in your mailing
3. TEST, TEST, TEST.

The one sure way to learn direct mail is to "adapt" someone else's success. I'm not sure it's possible to learn how to be successful without looking at junk mail very closely. The reason is that very few successful direct mailers will teach you about their success because they want to protect what they think are their business secrets. But all you have to do is save your junk mail, and, once a month or once a year, examine it carefully. At these times you should ask yourself why one choice was made over another. You may not be able to decide, but you will at least be setting the boundaries of the problem for yourself.

I'm trying to do that in this section. I want you, when you finish, to have some idea of the kinds of choices that are available to you when you think about direct mail. But you could get this all for yourself if you just save your junk mail.

You should know that all the third class and non-profit organization mail you receive is successful. You know because direct mail is very costly, and, as a result, all successful mailings have been extensively tested before you get them. Have no fear that you are receiving a test. The chances of that happening to you are less than .5 per cent, because testing is done on so limited a basis. And there is a lot to learn from successful junk mail.

The greatest single point you can learn from junk mail is involvement. *Involvement!* Involve the reader in your mailing. The best mailing pieces are the most involving ones. This can mean simply more parts in the direct mail piece. It may mean large, colorful, fold-out brochures. It can mean gripping copy in a letter, or it can mean an outside envelope of unusual size. It may mean all of these things or none. Sometimes involvement is created by simplicity itself: For example, just a card which says, "Yes, I've read about the people of Biafra and I want to help. Enclosed is my basic support check for $10.00." To say more might be unnecessary.

The last rule in direct mail is: Be cautious. Test everything possible. Test different types of postage; test different sizes of envelopes; test different letters; test different times of the year; test different approaches; test different lists. When you're sick of testing, test some more. There should be no end to your testing. Remember that there are many people who would like you to think that they know what you should do, but no one can be absolutely sure what will happen if you do it. Before you go out and spend your next $45,000 to follow someone's off-the-cuff suggestion, remember to TEST, TEST, TEST.....

How to speak the language, or what should you say in direct mail?

The big impulse in direct mail, as in every fund-raising method, is to talk about yourself and your needs. If you're going to build a wing on the hospital, it seems natural to have a brochure that includes pictures of the wing, floor plans, lists of the equipment to go inside, costs of each room, and costs of the pieces of equipment. Other "naturals" to be included are lengthy discussions of the "campaign plan," a letter from the general chairman, lengthy discussions of the total campaign goal and lots of space on the board of directors. Very little time is spent discussing why the wing should be built; what purpose it will achieve. Almost no time is spent asking the reader if he agrees with the project. Instead, the specifics of the project are discussed. Very little time is spent discussing the reason for the project.

You need to find the area of most agreement among the readers of your direct mail. If you represented Tugalong Hospital, you would need to spend a lot of time talking about specific cases: Penny Sue, who was hit by a car when she ran into the street to get her volley ball; Aunt Pauline, who would have died if the constant heart care center had not been opened two weeks before. "Do you think more lives should be saved like Penny Sue's and Aunt Pauline's? Send your check to us today."

It's not that you shouldn't discuss the architecture, floor plans, campaign plan and costs. It's just that you shouldn't spend so much time and take up so much space talking about them. Remember that many people may disagree with the details of the project, but few would disagree with helping Penny Sue and Aunt Pauline. Find the area of most agreement and stand on it with both feet. Talk about it until the cows come home.

Re-read the chapter on fund-raising psychology. Follow those ideas in direct mail. The main point is: Find a person who is capable of giving to you. Find out what problems he has, then tell him why your project will help him solve his problems.

What are the pieces in a direct mailing?

It's possible to have only one piece in a direct mailing and still have it do the job. This is called a self-mailer. At the other extreme, there is almost no limit to the number of pieces you can have. I have seen several with eight, nine, and ten pieces. In general, however, there are five major ones. They are:

1. Outside envelope
2. Letter
3. Brochure
4. Response card (gift card)
5. Return envelope

If you had to guess, which would you say was the most important? It's the response card or gift card. It's really quite understandable when you think about it, because this is where the action is. This is the spot the reader gets to say, "Yes, I agree with you," or "No, I don't agree with you, but please keep me informed about any other ideas you have in this area." The response card is where he gives his opinion, and from his point of view, that's the most important part. And since you want his response, this should be the most important part to you, too. It's literally where the action is.

What should you do about the response card's being the most important piece?

1. Make it a separate piece in the mailing. Many fund-raisers put the response card on the flap of the return envelope. This is the worst spot if you want it to stand out. And you do want it to stand out if you think it is the most important piece.

2. Make it a different shape and size than any other piece. This is to make it stand out more. Avoid the postcard size. It's good to make it the largest piece in the mailing so it will stand out. Sometimes it's good to have it folded once or twice. Large fold-out pieces frequently encourage involvement.

3. Print it on the strongest color paper in the mailing and use a bold color of ink. Avoid printing it on white paper unless it is the only white piece. It should stand out. People should notice it.

4. One sure way to improve the response to almost any mailing piece is to increase the type size on the response card by 50 per cent. It gets more attention that way, and since it's the most important piece, that's exactly what should happen. Also, you should make it easy to read by using both capital letters and small letters rather than all capitals or all small letters.

5. Offer as many choices as you can on it. Use the Cafeteria Theory rather than the Limited Menu Theory. You will get more responses the more choices you offer. Encourage as many different levels of giving as you can think of.

6. Never print anything on the back of the sheet. If you want it to be read, print only on one side. If you fold the response card, make sure it is print-side out. Do not hide your most important point. Make it difficult to avoid reading.

7. If possible, make sure the reader's name and address are on it. Somehow, he is drawn to reading his own name. Involve him.

8. Put "Yes" statements there. And check-boxes. Both are involving for the reader. What's a "Yes" statement? Example: "☐ YES! I'd like to see more homeless animals cared for by the Heartless Humane Society. Enclosed is my basic support check for $10.00." Try to think of as many "Yes" statements as you can.

9. Try putting a thick, bold rule around the edge of the card. It will get more attention. Fancy borders and certificate forms add impact. When possible, use photos.

10. Be sure to have different and interesting names for each level of giving. Test show the more levels of giving, the more gifts.

Because the response card is the most important piece in the mailing, the other pieces should be secondary. Their only reason for existing is to "feed" the reader into the response card. They should be smaller in size, calmer in color and less attention-getting.

But before we talk about the inside pieces, let's look at the outside.

Many direct mail experts feel the outside envelope is the most important piece in the mailing. They say, "If a person doesn't open the mailing, it doesn't matter what you've said inside." And, of course, that's true—as far as it goes. Studies show that only 90 per cent of all third class mail gets delivered. This is because 10 per cent of the addresses have either moved away or died. Of the 90 per cent that gets delivered, only 80 per cent gets opened. Another 10 per cent are not interested in looking inside. It is this 10 per cent that you hope to influence by careful attention to details on the outside envelope. It is important to do this, but remember that 80 per cent *do* look inside. So you should spend the most time there.

There are five points for you to consider in the outer envelope.

1. *General appearance*. You have several basic choices here. You can look like any of these four kinds of mail:

a.) Personal letters
b.) Bills
c.) Magazines and newspapers
d.) Junk mail

What kind gets the biggest response? Personal letters, of course. But the trouble is, it's very expensive. Envelopes need to be hand-addressed and hand-stamped. Usually the increase in cost is not worth it. It's cheaper and easier to look like a bill. Use a window envelope and a postage meter for stamps, and most people will open the envelope.

But be sure to avoid looking like junk mail.

2. *Paper shape, and size.* You should avoid the standard number 10 size white business envelope. It is a symbol of junk mail. Readers think this is "ordinary" and will not look inside. You should use warm, personal colors like ivory and beige. Using either larger or smaller outer envelope than number 10 is involving. It is unusual. The reader will open it to find out what's inside. The cost of other size envelopes is surprisingly small. Call your envelope supplier and check.

3. *Return address.* There are three basic choices here. You can use your charity's return address. This is the most common, and should always be used with mailings to donors because they want to read mail from you. Another choice is to leave off your charity name, but leave on the street address, city, state and zip. This is useful in mailings to people who don't know your charity because they will open the envelope to see who it's from. The last choice is to use different sender with a different address other than your own. Don't automatically have the Executive Director or President of the Board send the mailing. Consider using a famous person; his home or business address on the outer envelope which will arouse curiosity and frequently increase the response. If you are trying to look like a bill, try using an address in the downtown business section of your town. Also, if you're trying to look like a bill, be sure to include the words "Address Correction Requested" under the return address. This should be included as standard practice on all mailings to donors, because you don't ever want to loose a donor name and address.

4. *Whom you're sending it to.* The best way to address the envelope is to hand-type or hand-write each name and address. The only trouble is, this takes a lot of time and is very costly. To save money, many charities use labels, but labels are a symbol of junk mail. A much better choice is to use a window envelope and have the name and address on the response card that shows through the window. This gives the look of a bill, and the mailing is much more likely to be opened.

5. *Postage.* The whole question of postage is quite complex. Just to show you the dimensions of the problem, here are some of the major choices you have:

- a.) 1.7 cents (non-profit postage) printed permit. This is used most often in very large mailings (10,000-plus) because it's the cheapest way. Its main drawback for fund-raisers is that it's not forwarded if the person has moved, and so there's a lot of waste.

b.) 1.7 cent meter stamp. Put on by a postage meter.

c.) 2 cent stamp pre-cancelled. Pre-cancelled postage stamps have cancellation lines and postmarks already printed on them when you buy them, so the post office does not have to cancel each piece separately. They're not often used by charities because they don't know about them. They frequently get superior results for the mailing. Pre-cancelled stamps are sold at the post office.

d.) Two pre-cancelled 1 cent stamps. Same as above. The trouble with stamps is they are expensive to put on. Test to see whether the extra cost is justified in your case.

e.) 10 cent (first class) printed permit. First class is forwarded if the person has moved.

f.) 10 cent meter stamp. Put on by postage meter. Used primarily on bills and business letters. This is frequently the best solution to the postage problem.

g.) 10 cent stamp. Standard 10 cent stamps in rolls can be put on envelopes by machine. You should try them.

h.) 10 cent commemorative stamp. Commemorative stamps are unusual and are involving. The trouble, again, is that they must be put on by hand.

i.) 10 cent jumbo commemorative stamp. Larger-than-normal stamps also attract more attention. Must be hand-applied, but results are usually much better. You should try them even if you try no other.

j.) Ten 1 cent stamps. You'd be surprised how many people open letters with eight 1 cent stamps on them. The trouble is, you can't use that technique every time. 1 cent stamps can be put on by machine.

k.) Five 2 cent stamps. High level of involvement, as above. They may also be put on by machine.

l.) Air mail stamp (13 cents). Try using them on local mail. They get more attention.

m.) Special delivery (60 cents). Spectacular for giving a sense of urgency to an appeal. Should only be used with givers who have given $25 and over. Be sure to justify the cost in the letter by explaining the urgency.This is extremely effective once—it can't be used often.

n.) Registered mail (95 cents-plus). Same impact as special

delivery. Do you know anyone who could help opening a registered or special delivery letter?

6. *Words on the outside envelope.* "Have a Heart" or "Easter Seals Inside" are words on the outside of the envelope known as "teaser copy." They are used to increase interest and involvement, but, as a general rule, don't use them. They are a symbol of junk mail. They are usually only valuable for mass appeal charities. But consider using the words "first class," "air mail," and "special delivery" whenever you can. Also effective sometimes is "telegram," or, at election time, "referendum enclosed." Do some experimenting.

Once you've gotten past the outside envelope, there are even more problems and choices. Let's look at the return envelope first. It is normally dull and drab, and no one takes an interest in it. But care must be taken here, too. The most frequent error made on return envelopes is in the area of postage. Many charities require the reader to supply his own stamp or say, "A 10 cent stamp placed on this envelope will save us 12 cents." Both of these choices are terrible because they lose donors who don't have a stamp handy. This is also "penny-ante" and even destructive because it calls the reader's attention to an unimportant matter. Charities that do this are being cheap in ways that don't matter. Usually the savings on postage costs could be wiped out by simply getting one more donor you wouldn't otherwise have gotten.

Always, always use "business reply mail" and pay the 12 cents for each return. But don't make it a number six standard white business return envelope. Try a warm color, such as beige, suntan or putty, and make the size anything but the standard size.

Sometimes it's helpful to address the return envelope to "Mrs. Patsy Thrash" at address of your charity so the donor gets the feeling of talking to a person instead of a cold institution. Involvement is often stimulated by having "teaser copy" on the outside of the return envelope, such as, "My Love Plan Gift Is Inside." What's wrong on the outside envelope may not be wrong inside!

Most of your thinking about letters is probably all wrong. Wrong because you haven't thought enough about what they're supposed to do in relation to the other pieces in the mailing and also because you overemphasize their importance. You spend too much time writing them, when you should spend more of that time thinking about how to make the response card more involving.

Letters are not the place to explain your charity, talk about your programs, talk about your goals, talk about what you've done, or even talk about your strongest appeal.

Since it is often read first, the letter should be the place to tell the reader what's in the rest of the mailing. Specifically, it should direct him to the response card and urge him to act. A good rule of thumb is to mention the response card at least three times. The first time should be in the first paragraph, when you tell the reader you want him to make a gift and direct him to use the response card. Do not waste valuable time building an elaborate web that ends with your asking for the gift. Always ask for the gift in the first paragraph. Then spend the rest of the letter supporting the request.

Another way to tell him about the response card is to outline the different response choices in the letter. The third way to tell him about the response card is to give him exact instructions for responding, and urge him to act now. If you do not urge him to act now he may forget to act at all. If you have a deadline, you should emphasize it strongly.

If you have any space left after talking about the response card, you may mention your appeal. But you should talk about specific cases rather than the appeal in general. Try personalizing it whenever possible. For example: instead of saying, "We treat two thousand patients a month at Tugalong Hospital," you should talk about individuals like Penny Sue and Aunt Pauline.

Also you should use personal words when you talk about the donor's gift. "Your $10.00 will help another child like Penny Sue not be crippled for the rest of her life." Or, "Your $100.00 will help another patient like Aunt Pauline get a heart pacer."

You must be sure to talk about the donor himself, his needs, and how they can be fulfilled by him making a gift. Tell him what philosophies and emotions he can fulfill by giving; tell him what recognitions he will receive (in a listing of donors or on a bronze plaque); or tell him what product he will get if it's a fulfillment offer.

When you write your letter, remember that direct mail is weak. Try to compensate for this by making your words especially strong. In direct mail, being subtle is the same as not making the point at all. And don't worry about offending people, either. For every person you offend, you will wake up ten or twelve others and make them pay attention to what you're saying.

Never write a letter without a "P.S." Many people read the "P.S." first, and if they like it, they read the rest of the letter. So the best "P.S." is an intriguing, but incomplete statement that can only be understood by reading the rest of the letter. Here is a good one from the Tugalong Animal Humane Society, "P.S.: In the time it took you to read these words, three stray dogs died a terrible death from starvation."

You also need to think about the paper color, ink color, paper size and shape. Throw out your 8½″ × 11″ standard white stationery with black or blue printing! Or use it only when you write to suppliers for business reasons. Standard envelopes and standard stationery look standard and do not encourage involvement.

For fund-raising, use a different size, different color, think about a different shape, and don't use black ink. Using warm paper tones like ivory and beige matching the outside envelope is very good. Call a paper supply house and have them bring you some samples. You'll be surprised how many choices there are if you haven't looked in a while. Consider using a paper with a textured finish, because this adds interest to the mailing at surprisingly low cost. Try a warm brown ink instead of black or blue. (But it's O.K. to use blue in the signature.) A good size for many letters is 6″ × 9″, to make them look more personal.

The most important question about your letterhead is whether you should use it. Sometimes you get much better results if you make up the stationery for the occasion and make it seem to be someone's personal letter paper. Special fund-raising appeals call for separate letterheads. For example, a university might use "The Class of 1964," "The Alumni Fund," "The Capital Campaign for the Seventies," and "The President's Club," and even send all four to the same donor! Don't hesitate to be imaginative with the letterhead.

In other words, don't simply use the letterhead you have on hand. Think long and hard about having it redesigned to give it more impact. By all means, remove the names of the Board of Directors and other people from the left margin of your stationery. Unless one or more of those people are known by the person who looks at the letter, the names will act as a stumbling block for him to become a donor. He won't want to join an organization in which he doesn't know anyone. Only charities in which social climbing may be a strong reason for giving should use the Board Member list. In this case, the donor wants to know whom he's rubbing shoulders with. But if your board won't let you remove their names, try putting them on the back of the letter. This is becoming more and more popular with many charities.

Experiment with your next mailing by having a picture printed on the stationery. If it's emotional and involving, it will frequently cause more people to read the letter. You might also try putting in the picture of the person who is sending the letter, but make sure it's not a "mug" shot that is stiff and posed. A laughing or crying picture is good.

Talk to the reader more personally in the opening words. Instead of saying "Dear Friend," say "Dear Music Lover" or "Dear Democrat" or "Dear Neighbor." The best letter is, of course, the most personal, and you should avoid as many "Dear Friend" words as possible.

Try sending out all of your letters individually typed. Without a doubt, this will bring your best response. Some organizations do this with volunteer labor, an excellent use of the volunteer's time, because it creates more money for the charity. It is also very effective to have the recipients of the service of the charity send their own individual letters asking for gifts. In the case of a university, this would be the present students writing to alumni for gifts. In these cases, it is even more effective to have the letters handwritten.

Even if you can't hand-write or hand-type every letter you send out, you can, at least, hand-write a "P.S." or include a handwritten cover note. If you're sending out 100,000 letters, this might become a bit tiresome, so you could have the handwriting photo-copied and printed. A cover note is usually a separate piece of paper, perhaps 2″ × 3″, attached by paper clip or staple to the letter. This is usually very costly, so you might consider simulating the appearance of a cover note by having it printed on the letter itself. The idea behind the cover note is that a person other than the sender of the letter thinks the letter is important and urges the reader to look at it carefully and act on it.

Should letters be long or short? Partly because I'm better at writing short letters, and partly because I think people don't have much time to read long letters, I usually say short letters are better. But that's not necessarily true. That's just my bias. Actually, long letters are the best, but they are more difficult to write. The reason is that the letter loses its impact if it tries to discuss too many subjects. So a long letter, to be good, must restrict itself to making just a few strong points that are closely connected. The trick in a long letter is to make the same point in as many different ways as possible, and that is very difficult to do. Long letters are best when they are good, but most long letters try to make too many points and are bad.

The last piece in the mailing is the brochure. I've saved it till last because I hate it. The chief question you should ask yourself in any mailing is whether you should even include a brochure. I believe the one sure way to improve almost any mailing is to leave out the brochure. The reason is very simple. A good brochure, when it is good, is fine. But most brochures are bad, and when they are bad, they are terrible. And damaging. Even devastating!

The brochure is where you normally explain your charity and your activities and programs to the reader. You do this because you assume he wants to know about these activities, but that's a mistake on your part. He usually doesn't. Actually, the brochure forces him to look at things he's not interested in, and when you do this, you encourage him to find something to disagree with. Someone who may be quite interested in and excited about the work of the Little Sisters of the Poor may violently disagree with a specific, controversial program that might be in the brochure. Then they would not give.

When you talk to anyone about any subject, you are automatically selective. You don't tell them everything, if only because there isn't enough time. If you agree that you choose what you tell others, I simply recommend that you tell them all the things you think they'll agree with. When you first meet someone, you don't take a lot of time pointing out your warts and pimples. Instead, you try to look and act your best, emphasizing your strong points instead of your weak ones.

What are the good things you can do in a brochure?

1. *Interviews with donors.* One of the outstanding things you can do is to have interviews with present donors who describe why they made a gift. Especially effective are interviews with a wide variety of people—men, women, young, old, poor and rich. This gives the reader a great chance to find someone he can identify with. This is a very powerful involvement device.

2. *Photos that develop excitement and emotional involvement.* One of the best ways to make a brochure a big plus in a mailing is to use many big, clear photos that are emotionally exciting and involving. If you need captions for the photos, keep the number of words to a minimum and be sure the words add impact to the photos.

3. *Use the brochure to tell the story of one person who was helped by the charity.* This story should get the sympathetic involvement of the reader. It is possible to talk about more than one person in a brochure, but that sometimes causes the piece to lose impact.

4. *Give the reader a test.* Give him twenty questions to answer, with choices for him to check off. Tell him if he gets a score of at least fourteen, he should join your organization. Tell him in advance that if he gets a score of less than fourteen, he should *not* join. This simple idea has an amazing ability to involve the reader. But be sure that you don't make the test so hard that no one can pass! The test should include the beliefs that most of your present members share. Your goal should be to allow a marginal prospect to pass with flying colors.

5. *Tell the reader about the product he can buy.* If this is a fulfillment offer or product purchase, use the brochure to sell the benefits of the product for him. Sell the benefits.

6. *Give the reader some useful information.* A drug clinic could send out a brochure called, "How to Tell if Your Child Is not Using Drugs." Many churches, hospitals and universities send out pamphlets like "23 Things You Know About Wills that Aren't True." Consider educating and informing the reader about something that he's interested in. Sending a calendar of events in your charity is also useful, because he may keep it and come to one of your events later. Even if he doesn't give you a gift right away, this can be a technique for involving him further.

There are many other pieces that can be included in your mailing besides these five basic ones, and you should try to add as many as possible whenever you can. Frequently, your response rate will be greatly increased simply by adding a membership card or membership decal.

Try to change your mailings often by adding something unusual. The key to direct mail is keeping the reader interested, and variation is one way to do that. This is the best list of ideas I've come across. I hope it helps you the next time you get stuck for an idea.

THINK ABOUT MAILINGS THAT USE UNUSUAL STOCKS[1]:

1. Graph paper
2. Day-glo paper (red-letter day)

[1] From *Planning & Creating Better Direct Mail* by Yeck and Maguire. Copyright © by McGraw-Hill Inc. Used with permission.

3. Wallpaper
4. Sandpaper
5. Pressure-sensitive post card
6. Cloth
7. Wood . . . ⅛-inch plywood . . . paper
8. Aluminum foil
9. Transparent paper (cellophane, etc.)
10. Translucent paper (carbon copy, etc.)
11. Blotting paper
12. Phonograph record
13. Ribbon that talks a message when you run your thumbnail over it
14. Cork
15. Canvas
16. Wood veneer

THINK ABOUT USING UNUSUAL SHAPES, SIZES, DESIGN, OR FOLDS:

1. Simulated IBM card
2. Simulated membership card
3. Giant letter, telegram, or card
4. Circular (round in shape) letter
5. Letter or card die-cut into the shape of some object
6. Formal invitation (regular size, giant, or miniature)
7. Triple post card, with address showing, plain or die-cut
8. "Snap-box" which snaps into a cube when opened
9. Fold 8½ × 11 inch sheet longways for self-mailer
10. Trim a single-fold piece a little narrower at the fold to give it a butterfly look when opened
11. Deck of cards—fifty-two messages
12. Train-ticket format
13. Yellow page of phone book format
14. Simulated entertainment poster (movie, variety show, opera, ballet, hillbilly)

THINK ABOUT DIE CUTS, PUNCHING, DEFACING IN YOUR MAILINGS:

1. Pop-ups
2. Cards cut to special design
3. Circular (round in shape) letter, or zigzag letter

4. Envelope: die-cut all the way through to let color show through on both sides
5. Punch hole in paper and make it apply to message
6. Burned-edge letter
7. Pre-erased letter
8. Half letter: Cut the overrun of a previous letter in half, and on blank side write a short letter which may start, "Maybe we got only half of our story across to you."

THINK ABOUT UNUSUAL LAYOUTS:

1. Reverse letter (to be read in mirror)
2. Upside-down letterhead
3. Fancy reply cards or envelopes
4. Four-page letter or self-mailer
5. Handwritten letter or note
6. Shorthand on letter or envelope
7. Imitation telegram or imitation phone message
8. Music and words to a song
9. Stock certificates
10. Jigsaw puzzle
11. Name of letter-writer in top position on letterhead; company name subordinated
12. Format of "wanted" signs in post office, using fingerprints and front and profile photos to introduce salesmen—"Watch For This Man . . ."
13. Calendar page used as a memo (handwritten), but printed on a card stock and used as a mailing card
14. Magazine cartoons (reprinted with permission), used as a source of inexpensive but effective art
15. A photo used to fill the whole top fold of the letter, 8½″ × 11″ sheet; then accordion fold used, leaving the picture the first thing you see
16. In place of letterhead, attention-getting picture—no letterhead at all
17. Page out of dictionary
18. Wedding or party invitation
19. Label from bottle or can
20. Empty cigarette package

21. Instruction tag
22. Candy wrapper
23. Ticker tape
24. Yellow paper from wire service, like AP
25. Last will and testament
26. Child's building block
27. Garden seed packet
28. Page from foreign language dictionary
29. Insurance policy
30. Claim check
31. Birth certificate
32. Passport
33. Savings book (bank or savings-and-loan)
34. 3″ × 5″ recipe card
35. Sheet music
36. Map
37. Ad reprint
38. Magazine covers
39. Recipe
40. Menu
41. Paint paddles
42. Checkbook
43. Shelf paper
44. Printed sticker or decal
45. Credit card
46. Gift wrapping
47. Place mats or coasters
48. Crepe paper and streamers
49. Paid bill
50. Shoe or cereal box
51. Instruction sheets
52. Sheet of trading stamps
53. Paper towels
54. Soap box
55. Napkins
56. Roll of film wrapper—with spool print on inside of paper—to be unrolled as film

57. Adding machine tape
58. An offbeat greeting card
59. Film positive
60. Silk screen on wallpaper or cloth
61. Overprint in bright color on old telephone directory pages
62. Sheet of sandpaper or emery cloth
63. Giant shipping label (like one on product)
64. Overprint on company form (credit memo)
65. Paper party hat
66. Cardboard milk carton
67. Christmas wrapping paper
68. Kite paper
69. Newspaper mat (copy reversed)
70. Embossing on thin metal (like name plate or even packaging stickers)
71. Printing on a piece of building material (aluminum, floor tile, felt paper, etc.)
72. Lobster or spaghetti bib, big coaster, etc.
73. Printing on wrapper that goes around product
74. White shipping or mailing bag
75. Plastic bag
76. Corrugated packing board
77. Zipper reply card

THINK ABOUT UNUSUAL COPY STYLE:

1. Radio, TV, or movie script
2. Shorthand notes on envelope or on a tip-on addressed to the secretary
3. Telegram format and style
4. Newspaper clipping
5. News ticker
6. "*Time* style"

THINK ABOUT USING SPECIAL PROCESSES:

1. Invisible ink
2. Burning message
3. Fragrance

4. Cabala (erasable) process
5. Fingerprints
6. Wet message

THINK ABOUT ADDING SOMETHING UNUSUAL:

1. Gadgets
   a.) Glimericks
   b.) Vari-view
   c.) Gold-plated items
   d.) Flower seeds
   e.) Three-dimensional paste-on
   f.) Plastic gadget on post card, catalogue, or reply card
   g.) Useful item which becomes gift when removed
   h. to z.) (Their number is legion.)
2. Photos
   a.) Snapshots
   b.) Postage-stamp size
3. Foreign money
4. Fragrance
5. Special stamp
   a.) "First-day cover" on envelope
6. Special seals
   a.) With ribbons attached for important announcements

THINK ABOUT USING UNUSUAL CONTAINERS:

1. Tubes
2. Bags
3. Shape-conforming plastic
4. Cellophane envelopes, tubes, or bags
5. "Zip-velope"
6. Double-window envelope
7. Boxes (unusual)
8. Plastic bottle

THINK AROUT UNUSUAL MAILING PROCESSES:

1. Foreign mailings
2. Special postmarks

3. Messenger-boy delivery
4. Registered letters

THINK ABOUT USING SPECIALIZED STOCK MATERIAL AVAILABLE:

1. Printed personalized calendars and other "reminder advertising" material
2. Texas bucks, safety bucks, magic bucks, and the like
3. Flash cards
4. Zip envelopes with tag attachments
5. Bordered blanks
6. Giant letter or wire
7. Global letter
8. Holiday letterhead
9. Colorful-stock letterhead
10. Double-window envelopes
11. Zip envelopes with stock art

THINK ABOUT REPLY CARDS:

1. Two-color
2. Product or object in light half-tone screen behind the copy
3. Stylized art
4. Extra small or extra large cards
5. IBM card punched
6. Check squares in reverse (white in color band or color square to check)
7. Very large type, one-line signature
8. Two-color underlining of copy
9. Plastic mailbox on reply card
10. Smith-Corona, London, used a carrier pigeon as a reply device and got 100 per cent return.

THINK ABOUT ENVELOPE IMPACT:

1. Die-cut all the way through, so color of enclosure shows both front and back
2. Pennies showing through double window. ("The price is $1.98 . . . Send us $2. . . . Here's your change.")
3. Put a shorthand note on the envelope or on a tip-on addressed to the secretary
4. Photograph on back of envelope repeated inside as letterhead

THINK ABOUT UNUSUAL ART:

1. Enlarged sections of photographs
2. Surrealistic art
3. Child's drawings
4. Doodles
5. Three-dimensional art
6. Photographs of puppets

Mailing lists

When I asked you which piece in the mailing was most important, I was being sly. I didn't include the most important piece: the mailing list. Many direct mail people feel that nothing you say inside can make up for sending it to the wrong person, and it is certainly true that this is a very critical area.

There are two major resources in the field of mailing lists. One is *Direct Mail List Rate and Data*, which is a directory of over 21,000 lists which are available for rent. It has over twenty pages of lists of donors to other charities you may rent! Most libraries have a copy of this book, and, if you'd like to have a copy in your office, the price is $50.00 per year. It is a publication of Standard Rate and Data Service. However, you should be aware that this directory is not a complete listing of all available lists. Many of the best lists avoid being listed here.

Where are they listed? With the next major resource in the field—list brokers. List brokers are people who "rent" lists to anyone who wants them. They charge only the list owner (not you) for this service, so, in effect, it's free to you. A major reason for you to use a list broker is that he has a lot of experience in judging which lists are best under what conditions, and this is something you can't get by looking in *Direct Mail List Rate and Data*. One of the difficulties with list brokers, however, is that there aren't very many of them and they're located only in major cities (New York, Chicago and San Francisco). For a list of list brokers, look in *Direct Mail List Rate and Data*. A word of caution—deal only with the most reputable brokers. Check to be sure that he is a member of the Mailing List Broker's Association. One excellent broker who specializes in fund-raising lists for charities is Dick Hammond of Names in the News (California) Inc., based in San Francisco.

What types of mailing lists are the best lists for fund-raisers? You should judge all lists to see if they meet these needs. You need to know:

1. If a person opens his mail
2. If he reads his mail
3. If he buys by mail
4. What his interests are
5. If he donates by mail

Among the rental lists, the best list you can get is a list of donors to a similar charity. Here are the kinds of lists which should interest you (best lists first):

1. *Your own donor lists.* Undoubtedly the best people for you to solicit are people who've given to you before. They are strongly involved and interested in you and don't want to stop giving. Make mailings to them that are different from the mailings you send to prospects. Urge them to give more frequently and to give more.

2. *Your constituents.* People who've received the service you offer or who would benefit from your service at some point (e.g., people who live in the area served by a hospital) are very strong prospects for you to mail to. Caution! Many fund-raisers make the mistake of renting "mass" lists of people who live in nearby neighborhoods on the theory that they are constituents. Usually this is a mistake and the response will be low. Instead, try renting donors to other charities similar to your own and subscribers to magazines your donors might be likely to read.

3. *Donors to other charities.* If you don't have a ready-made list of constituents, this is the best list you can get. Some of these lists can be rented, but, in many cases, the only way you can get them is to exchange your list of donors for theirs. If you are not exchanging your donor list with other charities, you are missing an outstanding opportunity for the growth of your organization.

4. *Magazine subscriber lists.* Very good lists for fund-raisers because they show what interests the subscribers have. For example, *Psychology Today* may tell you they are concerned about people and *Ramparts* may tell you they're liberal. Frequently these two magazines get very high responses for charities. Many magazines also offer their expired subscribers for rent, and these will get a lower response but should be tested if the subscribers do well. The prices for magazine subscriber lists range from $25.00 per thousand names to $40.00 per thousand names.

5. *Mail order buyers*. The fact that these people have responded to direct mail makes these lists very important for you, regardless of the product they bought. Some lists that work well for fund-raisers are Ambassador Leather, the Kenton Collection, and Time-Life Books. You may select inquirers, multiple buyers, current buyers, and past buyers. Multiple buyers are the best, and you probably should not buy the inquirers. The rental charge is between $25.00 and $35.00 per thousand names.

6. *Retail customer and credit lists*. These lists are valuable because they indicate special interests and characteristics of the customers. Typically, the best lists are not available for rent but may be gotten as a "donation" from some stores. A variation on this is to ask department stores to include your solicitation letter in their next billing to all their customers. This usually insures that it will be read at least. When the lists can be rented, the cost is $25.00 to $35.00 per one thousand names.

7. *Travel card lists*. Fairly good response rates for fund-raisers. Typical lists are American Express, Diners Club and Carte Blanche. Be sure to allow donations to be charged to the credit card involved. The rental cost is $30.00 to $40.00 per one thousand names.

8. *Occupational lists*. From here on, the lists become more and more useless to fund-raisers. The reason is because we don't know anything about the person on the list, especially whether he responds to direct mail. Typical lists in this category include doctors, lawyers, executives, professors, teachers and owners of small businesses. As a general rule, avoid these lists. The costs run $25.00 to $45.00 per one thousand names.

9. *Business lists*. Usually not addressed to specific persons, just a job title (such as "President" or "Comptroller") at a company. Low response rates. Avoid! Costs run $25.00 to $35.00 per one thousand names.

10. *Life-stage and life-event lists*. Categories in these lists include new residents, senior citizens, teenagers, new parents, college students, new brides, newly discharged veterans, and divorced persons. Occasionally useful to fund-raisers, but frequently such persons are preoccupied with problems of their own. The rental charge is $25.00 to $35.00 per one thousand names.

11. *Mass lists*. These are the worst lists for charities. They indicate

nothing about the persons on the list and they have tiny response rates. Such lists include occupants (no names, only addresses), telephone (if you have a telephone listed in your name), auto registration (if you own a car), and voter registration (if you are a registered voter). Many fund-raisers like these lists because they're cheap (sometimes free or $5.00 to $10.00 per thousand names or occasionally running as high as $35.00 per thousand names). But the cheapness should stop you. Here, as in so many places, you get what you pay for. Before attempting to use mass lists, you should test all the other categories of lists. That should take you about ten years.

Exchange your lists!

The most stupid and ridiculous policy I encounter in charities is the refusal to think about exchanging donor lists. Don't let this happen to you. Face the problem. Nine out of ten fund-raisers are against ever giving out their donor list for any reason, while the facts overwhelmingly support the logic of exchanges.

There are three main reasons why charities are afraid to exchange their donor lists.

1. *Fear of loss of donors.* Basically, you have a lack of confidence in your basic appeal when compared to the appeal of another charity. You feel that if you exchange your donors, the other charity will end up with your donors because of the other charity's better appeal. This is false and comes from not really understanding what you give your donors. By giving to you, they are fulfilling their needs, their self-images. And they are very protective of that and usually will not give up one charity to join another. What happens is they usually add a charity to their giving list.

But the fear of loss of donors is a psychological question in disguise. It's really an empirical question that can be answered by examining the facts. If charities actually lost donors in the process of exchanging, they would soon be out of business and they would not do it. The fact that there are many hundreds of thriving charities thaa do exchange their lists means that this is not the case. A way for you to really satisfy yourself on this point, however, is to call your list broker and ask him for three names of charities who exchange their donor lists. Then call each of the three and ask the executive director what his experience with loss of donors has been.

2. *Fear of invasion of donor privacy.* You are afraid that your donors, if they find out that you exchange their names with another charity, will be angry and will write you nasty letters. The facts are that the average person in the United States is on over two hundred mailing lists and receives over eight hundred pieces of junk mail a year. It is extremely unlikely that he would ever find out where his name came from on any particular mailing he receives. However, you can doubly guard against this possibility, when you exchange your lists, by altering the form of the donor's name (e.g., instead of Mrs. Paul Carson, use Mrs. P. Carson). It is also interesting that many charities who don't exchange their lists or even rent them, still get letters from angry donors accusing them of giving out their names. Obviously the donors don't know the true source.

But the best way to handle this objection is to tell all donors explicitly that you intend to exchange their names because the work of your charity is so important as to demand all the extra revenue you can get. Sometimes the way around this problem is to ask the donors for their permission. Then everyone's happy.

3. *Fear of loss of donors by theft.* In this case you can guard against this fear by dealing only with list brokers who know the reputations of the charities they deal with. Another thing you can do is "seed" the list with misspelled or even false names so you can detect unauthorized use. These false names are evidence in court, and it is a criminal offense to steal a list from a list owner.

But, of course, the main reason for exchanging donor lists is that they bring in more money for the charity than any other list (except the charity's own donor list). Let me illustrate this for you. Here is a comparison of the same mailing sent to three different lists. I have used a mass list, a magazine rental list and a donor exchange list. Please notice the bottom line.

	Calculation	Mass List	Magazine List	Donor Exchange List
Income				
1. Donor life	×	3	4	6
2. Average donation	×	$8.00	$13.00	$15.00
3. Increase ratio	×	1.2	1.3	1.6
4. 5% discount rate	=	.677	.677	.677

	Calculation	Mass List	Magazine List	Donor Exchange List
Income				
5. Future income from each donor+	×	$19.50	$45.77	$97.49
6. Average donation	=	$8.00	$13.00	$15.00
7. Income from each donor	×	$27.50	$58.77	$112.49
8. Donors (response rate)	=	6	11	20
9. Total income from 1,000 donors		$165.00	$646.47	$2,249.80
Expenses				
10. List rental per 1,000 pcs	+	$25.00	$30.00	0
11. Package and postage per 1,000 pcs	=	$87.00	$87.00	$87.00
12. Total mailing expenses per 1,000 pcs		$112.00	$117.00	$87.00
Net Income (Profit) per 1,000 pieces				
9. Total income from 1,000 donors	−	$165.00	$646.47	$2,249.80
12. Total mailing expenses	=	$112.00	$117.00	$87.00
13. Net income (profit) per 1,000 pcs	×	$53.00	$529.47	$2,162.80
Total Income from All Prospects				
13. Net income (profit) per 1,000 pcs	×	$53.00	$529.47	$2,162.80
14. List universe	=	300,000	80,000	30,000
15. Total income from all prospects		$15,900.00	$42,357.60	$64,884.00

EXCHANGE YOUR LISTS!

4 Why you should not try to get foundation grants

If you took an opinion poll to find out where most people think money for charity comes from, I think they'd say "foundations." You'd probably find the same thought among fund-raising professionals. But this is dead wrong. Let's look at the facts:

1. Philanthropy in the United States is big business. In 1972, almost $23 billion was given away to charities (excluding government grants). Of this total, approximately 10 per cent was given by foundations. Direct mail giving was 50 per cent and giving through wills and bequests was 13 per cent.

2. There are 35,000 foundations in the United States, according to the latest IRS list. These foundations have only 1,000 paid full-time staff, with almost 750 in just four foundations!

3. Over half (56 per cent) of the grants foundations make are given in three areas: education, health and sciences. Social welfare grants amount to an additional 20 per cent of the total.

4. Foundation executives estimate that 60 to 80 per cent of the proposals they receive are rejected by them. They say most of these proposals don't fall within the stated interests of the foundation.

5. Most of the foundations are run by WASPs, who naturally continue their own interests. As a result, and despite many foundation's protests to the contrary, they're not very adventuresome or innovative. (See Waldemar Nielson's discussion of this point in his book *The Big Foundations.*)

What does all this mean? It means odds are stacked against you. Foundations have little staff to review your project, they're not very receptive to new or radical ideas, they reject many more proposals than they fund, and they give only 10 per cent of the total philanthropic dollars anyway!

What should you do under these circumstances? First, look at the situation pessimistically. Assume that little will come of your efforts. At worst, you will be getting an education on how funding sources work. And, at best, you will be pleasantly surprised by getting a grant. Second, if you are a person who, nevertheless, likes to cover all possibilities, resolve to spend only 10 per cent of your time trying to get money from foundations. In other words, put about as much time into it as you are likely to get money out of it. Third, try to carefully estimate your chances for success before you spend large amounts of time and money, needlessly.

In order to figure out how successful you'll be, you have to investigate a lot of sources.

1. *Foundation Directory*, Edition 4, 1971, Columbia University Press, $15. This is the main source of information of the "big" foundations (those with $500,000 or more in assets or those who made grants of $25,000 or more). Number of foundations listed: 5,454 out of the 35,000 total. So, 29,546 are not listed (these are the "small" foundations). Only grants made by 364 foundations are indexed by subject area.

2. *Foundation Grants Index*. Two editions of this are out. 1970-71 is a two-year combined listing of more than 17,000 grants (of $10,000 or more). The 1972 edition has more than 10,000 grants listed (also of $10,000 or more). Both editions index grants by subject fields (area of interest). Available from Columbia University Press. $10.

3. *Foundation Grants Data Bank*. This is a computer print-out of grants by topic area and is available in two forms. One, the Foundation Center and the regional depositories have some print-outs on hand of general topics. Here is a list of topics you will find as of mid-1974:

Preliminary list of possible topics for grant print-outs

1. Elementary and secondary education (public)
2. Elementary and secondary education (private)
3. Pre-school and day-care projects
4. Adult education
5. Personnel development (career training; para-professionals, etc.)
6. Higher education endowment
7. Higher education scholarships, fellowships and loans
8. Higher education buildings and equipment
9. Educational innovation and research (on all levels)
10. Educational media (TV, film, radio)
11. Libraries (all types); bibliography
12. Black institutions of higher education
13. Scholarships, fellowships and loans for minority groups and women
14. Medical research
15. Mental health
16. Hospitals
17. Health agencies
18. Medical care and rehabilitation (excluding drugs and alcoholism)
19. Drugs and alcoholism (research and rehabilitation)
20. Fine arts (painting, sculpture, etc.)
21. Music
22. Dance
23. Theatre
24. Media
25. Geographic breakdown of all international grants by country
26. Physical sciences (include astronomy, chemistry, etc.)
27. Environmental research
28. Ecology and conservation
29. Social science research (include political science, sociology, psychology, etc.)
30. Law (research and legal-aid type projects)

31. Religious associations
32. Religious buildings (including churches, temples, etc.)
33. Religious education (both religious schools and schools affiliated with one religious group, by denomination, including theological education with theology)
34. Child welfare
35. Youth agencies (separate print-out for Y's and Boy and Girl Scouts)
36. Aged
37. Physically handicapped
38. Housing
39. Race relations (separate print-outs for improving race relations among Hispanics, Blacks, American Indians, etc.)
40. Delinquency, crime and prison reform

The second way you can use this information is to order a computer search for any specific subject area you may be interested in. The charge for this is $10 for the first 50 grant records and 10 cents for each one after that. These print-outs may be ordered directly from the Foundation Center. The Data bank contains approximately 22,000 grants of $10,000 or more (as of 1974). The Data bank is growing at the rate of 1500 grants every two months.

4. *The Foundation Grants Index.* This is a list of grants of $5,000 or more which is published six times a year, every two months, as a part of the *Foundation News.* The cost is $10 per year. Each year these reports are bound in the annual summary.

5. *The Foundation Center Information Quarterly.* This is an updating of the information in *The Foundation Directory*, including any changes in policy of the foundations and other pertinent changes. It also updates the *Foundation Annual Reports on Film,* and the *Foundation Grants Data Bank.* It lists new books, articles and other publications relating to foundations. The cost is $7.50 per year.

6. *The Foundation Center*, 888 Seventh Avenue, New York City. Hours: 10 A.M. to 5 P.M. weekdays only. Free. It is a library with nearly all the publicly available information on foundations on hand.

7. *Regional Reference Collection.* If you can't make it to New York City, the next best thing is to consult their collection closest to you. Some of their information is at:

Name	*Geographical Coverage*
The Associated Foundation of Greater Boston One Boston Place, Suite 948 Boston, Massachusetts 02108	Connecticut, Maine, Massachusetts, New Hampshire, Rhode Island, Vermont
Cleveland Foundation Library 700 National City Bank Building Cleveland, Ohio 44114	Delaware, District of Columbia, Maryland, New Jersey, Ohio, Pennsylvania, West Virginia
The Newberry Library 60 West Walton Street Chicago, Illinois 60610	Illinois, Indiana, Michigan, Minnesota, North Dakota, South Dakota, Wisconsin
Foundation Collection Marquette University Memorial Library 1415 West Wisconsin Avenue Milwaukee, Wisconsin 53233	Illinois, Indiana, Iowa, Michigan, Minnesota, Ohio, Wisconsin
The Danforth Foundation 222 South Central Avenue St. Louis, Missouri 63105	Iowa, Kansas, Missouri, Nebraska
Foundation Library Collection Atlanta Public Library 126 Carnegie Way, N.W. Atlanta, Georgia 30303	Alabama, Florida, Georgia, Kentucky, Mississippi, North Carolina, South Carolina, Tennessee, Virginia
Regional Foundation Library The Hogg Foundation for Mental Health The University of Texas Austin, Texas 78712	Arkansas, Louisiana, New Mexico, Oklahoma, Texas
Foundation Collection Reference Department	Alaska, Arizona, California, Colorado, Hawaii, Nevada,

Name	*Geographical Coverage*
University Research Library University of California Los Angeles, California 90024	Utah
San Francisco Public Library Business Branch 530 Kearny Street San Francisco, California 94108	Alaska, California, Colorado, Hawaii, Idaho, Montana, Nevada, Oregon, Utah, Washington, Wyoming
Foundation Center Collection Social Science Reference Thomas Hale Hamilton Library Honolulu, Hawaii 96822	California, Hawaii, Oregon, Washington
Library Association of Portland 801 S.W. Tenth Avenue Portland, Oregon 97205	Alaska California Hawaii Oregon Washington
Rochester Public Library Business and Social Sciences Division 115 South Avenue Rochester, New York 14604	New York
Oklahoma City Community Foundation 1300 North Broadway Oklahoma City, Oklahoma 73103	Oklahoma
Miami-Dade Public Library 1 Biscayne Boulevard Miami, Florida 33132	Florida

Name	*Geographical Coverage*
Business and Science Division New Orleans Public Library 219 Loyola Avenue New Orleans, Louisiana 70140	Louisiana
Minneapolis Public Library Sociology Department 300 Nicollet Mall Minneapolis, Minnesota 55401	Iowa Minnesota North Dakota South Dakota
American Alumni Council One Dupont Circle, Suite 530 Washington, D.C.	Membership Reference Collection—select returns
Chicago Community Trust 208 South La Salle Street Chicago, Illinois 60604	national collection
New Hampshire Charitable Fund 1 South Street Concord, New Hampshire 03301	New Hampshire
Director of University Libraries 271 Hillman Library University of Pittsburgh Pittsburgh, Pa. 15213	Pennsylvania
Linda Hall Library Reference Department 5109 Cherry Street Kansas City, Missouri 64110	Kansas Missouri
Kanawha County Public Library 123 Capitol Street Charleston, West Virginia 25301	West Virginia

Name	*Geographical Coverage*
The Public Library of Des Moines, Iowa Main Library 100 Locust Street Des Moines, Iowa 50309	Iowa
Laramie County Community College Library 1400 E. College Drive Cheyenne, Wyoming 82001	Wyoming
The Free Library of Philadelphia Logan Square Philadelphia, Pa. 19103	Delaware New Jersey Pennsylvania
Birmingham Public Library 2020 Seventh Avenue, North Birmingham, Alabama 35203	Alabama
Jacksonville Public Libraries 122 North Ocean Street Jacksonville, Florida 32202	Florida
Enoch Pratt Free Library 400 Cathedral Street Baltimore, Maryland 21201	Maryland
Boston Public Library Box 286, Z Boston, Massachusetts 02117	Massachusetts
Jackson Metropolitan Library 301 N. State Street Jackson, Mississippi 39201	Mississippi
New York State Library State Education Department Education Building Albany, New York 12224	New York

Name	*Geographical Coverage*
Hartford Public Library 500 Main Street Hartford, Connecticut 06103	Connecticut Massachusetts Rhode Island
Duke University Durham, North Carolina 27706	North Carolina
Seattle Public Library 1000 Fourth Avenue Seattle, Washington 98104	Washington
Henry Ford Centennial Library 15301 Michigan Avenue Dearborn, Michigan 48126	Michigan
Sociology Division Denver Public Library 1357 Broadway Denver, Colorado 80203	Colorado
Providence Public Library 150 Empire Street Providence, Rhode Island 02903	Rhode Island
The Grand Rapids Public Library Library Plaza Grand Rapids, Michigan 49502	Michigan
Salt Lake City Public Library 209 East 5th South Salt Lake City, Utah 84111	Utah
New Jersey State Library Reference Section 185 West State Street Trenton, New Jersey 08625	New Jersey

This list will soon be out of date, however. In 1974 the Foundation Center expects at least one Regional Reference Collection in every state. Write to them to find the one closest to you.

8. *Foundation Information Returns (IRS Forms 990 and 990 AR).* Both the Foundation Center and the Regional Reference Collections have two very important pieces of information: the Internal Revenue Service forms 990 and 990AR. The 990 form is the income tax form, showing income and expenditures. The 990AR is the annual report which all foundations are required to file yearly. In many cases, these IRS returns are the only source of information on many "small" or local foundations.

You may buy any you're interested in for 15 cents each on microfiche from the Foundation Center. If you wish to order all of the returns for foundations in your state, or in any other state, you may get them by writing the Director, Internal Revenue Service Center, PO Box 187, Cornwells Heights, PA 19020, The prices are:

State	*Price*	*State*	*Price*
Alabama	$31.00	Minnesota	$108.00
Alaska	2.50	Mississipi	17.00
Arizona	27.00	Missouri	119.00
Arkansas	27.00	Montana	11.00
California	433.00	Nebraska	34.00
Colorado	56.00	Nevada	6.00
Connecticut	135.00	New Hampshire	43.00
Delaware	35.00	New Jersey	137.00
District of Columbia	65.00	New Mexico	8.00
Florida	118.00	New York	1,137.00
Georgia	92.00	North Carolina	96.00
Hawaii	17.00	North Dakota	8.00
Idaho	8.00	Ohio	268.00
Illinois	360.00	Oklahoma	39.00
Indiana	104.00	Oregon	43.00
Iowa	58.00	Pennsylvania	316.00
Kansas	35.00	Rhode Island	28.00
Kentucky	32.00	South Carolina	30.00
Louisiana	44.00	South Dakota	7.00
Maine	25.00	Tennessee	50.00
Maryland	87.00	Texas	244.00
Massachusetts	304.00	Utah	20.00
Michigan	175.00	Vermont	11.00

State	*Price*	*State*	*Price*
Virginia	$ 80.00	Wyoming	$16.00
Washington	66.00	OIO (Office of International Operations)	16.00
West Virginia	12.00		
Wisconsin	139.00		

Complete Set: $5,379.50

9. *Foundation Annual Reports on Film.* The annual reports of the large national foundations are available on film, and can be ordered from the Foundation Center.

Series 1
Set of 198 foundation reports (111 fiche), 1970
Price: $25.00 per set; $1.00 per fiche

Series 2
Set of 96 foundation reports (52 fiche), October 1972
Price: $13.00 per set; $1.00 per fiche

Series 3
Set of 32 foundation reports (15 fiche), January 1973
Price: $4.00 per set; $1.00 per fiche

Series 4
Set of 33 foundation reports (17 fiche), April 1973
Price: $4.50 per set; $1.00 per fiche

Series 5
Set of 33 foundation reports (11 fiche), July 1973
Price: $3.00 per set; $1.00 per fiche

Series 6
Set of 113 foundation reports (57 fiche), October 1973
Price: $14.50 per set; $1.00 per fiche

Series 7
Set of 111 foundation reports (52 fiche), January 1973
Price: $13.00 per set; $1.00 per fiche

Series 8
Set of 39 foundation reports (23 fiche), April 1973
Price: $6.00 per set; $1.00 per fiche

To help you decide what you want to order, the Foundation Center has a free *Guide to Foundation Annual Reports on Film, 1970.* Other updates of the *Guide are in the Foundation Center Information Quarterly.*

10. *List of Organizations Filing as Private Foundation.* Contains the names and addresses of the 35,000 foundations. This list and the 990 and 990AR returns are the only sources of information on most of these foundations.

11. *Other publications.* Many foundations publish pamphlets or other pieces describing their program interests and, in some cases, the rules you should follow in applying for a grant from them. The Foundation Center and some of the Regional Reference Collections have these on file for you to examine. If you become interested in a particular foundation, you should write to them asking if they have any information available, and you should start your own file on them.

On the whole, it's pretty easy to find out if any of the "big" foundations might be interested in your specific project. Just look in four sources: *The Foundation Directory, The Foundation Grants Index, the Foundation Center Information Quarterly, and the Foundation News.* All of these should be at your local library. Then look up the annual report for each of the foundations you think might be interested in you. After reading that, you can decide how to proceed.

But if you only want a small amount of money, and you are basically a "local" kind of charity, you have a much more serious and time-consuming kind of problem. The place for you to begin is the *List of Organizations Filing as Private Foundations.* Foundations are listed there alphabetically within states, so all you can do is find out which foundations are near you. Then either visit a Regional Reference Collection or the Foundation Center itself (best because it has the most information) and read all of the annual reports for all the foundations in your state. This is obviously very time-consuming, but there is nothing else you can do.

But before you go rushing off: take a look at your chances for success. Here's an easy test that will tell you if you should spend time in this area. Ask yourself these questions and rate yourself accordingly. If you get over 75 points, you have a pretty good chance of being successful.

How to find out if you will be successful in getting foundation grants

1. *How similar are the stated purposes and goals of the foundations and the purposes and goals of your project?* Maximum score: 50 points. In order to answer this question well, you might ask yourself about these areas:

1. Does the foundation make grants for your kind of project?
2. Does the foundation make general grants to charities like yours?
3. Does the foundation make grants in your locale?
4. Does the foundation make grants for the type of gift you want? (i.e., operating deficit, construction, endowment or special projects outside of normal operations).

Each foundation you feel is a prospect for you should be rated by asking each of these four questions. Then rate each foundation on the following scale:

1. Not similar
2. Somewhat similar
3. Very similar

How many "very similar" foundations do you have?

☐ 10 or more (30 points)
☐ 9 or less (25 points)

How many "a little similar" foundations do you have?

☐ 20 or more (20 points)
☐ 19 or less (15 points)

2. *How well do you know the foundations you're applying to?* Maximum score: 30 points. (If you don't know anyone, you should start a project of getting to know the foundation staff. One helpful suggestion is to put people the foundation has either worked with or given grants to on your Board of Advisors for the project you want to fund.) Rate each foundation on the following scale:

1. No previous contact
2. Some contact with either their staff or board
3. Know them well

How many "know them well" foundations do you have?

☐ 10 or more (20 points)
☐ 9 or less (15 points)

How many "some contact with either their staff or board" foundations do you have?

☐ 20 or more (10 points)
☐ 19 or less (5 points)

3. *How much money do you think it might be possible to get from all these foundations if you were successful with all of them?* Maximum score: 10 points. Steps are:

1. Calculate the average grant size for each foundation. (This is done by finding out how much money they give away in one year; divide that figure by the total number of grants they made in that year. The result is the average grant for each foundation.
2. Add the average grants of each foundation. This is the total grants possible.
3. What is your project goal (in dollars)?
4. Figure the ratio of total grants possible to project goal (in dollars).

Then:

Is this amount:

- ☐ less than 50 per cent of your goal?
- ☐ 100 per cent of your goal?
- ☐ 200 per cent of your goal?
- ☐ 300 per cent of your goal?

4. *How much time will it take you?* Maximum score: 10 points. Here are three major areas for you to consider:

1. The research (both on the project and on the foundations). Estimate two to eight weeks for this task.
2. The proposal (the actual writing time). Estimate two to eight weeks for this task.
3. Time required for you to deliver the proposal personally to the foundation (be sure to count at least one week for this). Estimate one to three weeks for this task.

Then:

Is this amount of time:

- ☐ 5 weeks or less (10 points)?
- ☐ 6-10 weeks (5 points)?
- ☐ 11-19 weeks (3 points)?

5. *How much will it cost?* Maximum score: 10 points. There are four major cost areas. (Be sure to figure what you'd have to pay if you bought the service from an independent contractor.):

1. Research. Estimate a minimum of $500.
2. Proposal. Estimate a minimum of $500.
3. Take proposal to the foundations. Estimate a minimum of $500.
4. Other costs (including *overhead*, postage, paper, supplies, newsletter, annual report, other publications). Estimate a minimum of $500.

Add your estimates:

- ☐ $2,000 or less (10 points)
- ☐ $2,000 to $3,000 (5 points)
- ☐ more than $3,000 (3 points)

More suggestions on getting foundation grants

You should be aware of the fact that "big" foundations and "small" foundations expect different things from the charities they give money to.

"Big" foundations typically want projects with national impact and will not give to operating budgets or capital campaigns or endowments. Also, there is much information available on the interests of the big foundations. There isn't much guesswork about what they will fund and what they won't fund.

With the "small" foundations just the opposite is true. They want projects with local impact and they may give to operating budgets, capital campaigns or endowments. Also, there is hardly any information on their interests.

The "big" foundations are, as a rule, concerned with many of the following questions:

1. How long will your project take?
2. How much will it cost?
3. How will you measure the success of the project?
4. How will you finance the project after this grant? (It should be self-sufficient by the time initial funding ends.)

The "small" foundations have different standards. They will ask:

1. Does the problem this project is designed to answer need an answer?
2. Is this project capable of solving the problem?
3. What is the track record of the charity? (Has it solved other problems through other projects before?)
4. What is the reputation of the charity in its field?
5. Does the charity have the personnel to direct the project?
6. How realistic are the cost estimates?
7. How long will the project take?
8. How will you measure the success of the project?

There are two other implications of foundation grant-getting you should know about. First, usually the Executive Director will have to visit the foundation personally (even if you know someone on the staff or the board of directors). The reason is that foundations typically want to talk to the person who's going to spend the money, not the person who wrote the proposal.

Second, foundations will want to know what you're planning to do with the results. You might look at this as their wanting some mileage out of their money. Basically, they want some publicity. Suggestion: Do a written follow-up study on how well the project achieved its goals, then publish this and distribute it widely. Also, whenever you put out any news releases or publicity information about the project, be sure to mention this was all possible through the generosity of the particular foundation that funded you.

But, of course, the best way to get a foundation grant is to not follow this way at all. Take the marketing approach: find a foundation, then design a project they would be interested in funding.

Structuring your organization to maximize appeal to foundations

Here is the method I propose you follow:

1. Document your past successes with projects.
   a.) Have follow-up studies on hand.
   b.) Make a case presentation summarizing these projects.
2. Do research.
   a.) Find out what other organizations like yours received grants from foundations.
   b.) What those grants were for.
3. Draw upon internal operating plan (strategy plan).
   a.) Make list of good R & D fields (projects).
   b.) Decide who should be in charge of them (outside professionals or yourself?)
   c.) How much time should each project take?
   d.) How much will each project cost?
   e.) What are potential funding sources for each project?
4. Make plans for publishing/publicizing the results.
5. Indicate the specific results which will be achieved by this investment by the foundation.

a.) You must be able to answer the question for the foundation: "Why should we give money to you versus another charity in the same field?" Think about this question from the foundation's point-of-view: Where will the foundation's dollar do the most good?

6. Document your R & D track record to date.
7. Get an internal management report (whether good or bad). If you don't think the foundation will accept your opinion, get an outside impartial authority to make a report.
8. Say when your project will be self-supporting.

Most fund-raisers spend entirely too much time trying to write the best proposal possible. They make the fundamental mistake of thinking that the best written proposal is the best proposal. Writing the project down and then actually applying for the grant is a relatively simple process which I've outlined below.

How to apply

1. Do research on the foundations.
   a.) Find the area of mutual interest (the foundation's interests and your project's interests should match).
   b.) Amount of money you need.
2. Write proposal. Include:
   a.) Introduction (who you are in one sentence).
   b.) Project
   c.) Budget and finances
   d.) Personnel biographies
   e.) Endorsements
   f.) General organizational information (supporting material such as annual report, other project descriptions, etc.).
3. First contact/introductory letter (on one page).
   a.) Who we are (one sentence.)
   b.) Project (description and cost).
   c.) May we submit a proposal?
4. Replies.
   a.) If yes, call for appointment.
   b.) If no, send thank you letter.
   c.) If no answer—telephone.
5. Call for appointment.

6. Go see/take proposal/ask for their suggestions for improvement.
7. Revise proposal incorporating their suggestions.
8. Submit proposal.
9. Follow-up.

5 Down the campaign trail

The capital funds campaign is a special kind of fund-raising that is probably the cheapest way to raise a large amount of money. The trouble with it is that you must have a large number of volunteers in order to do this, and that means your cause must have wide-spread appeal or at least be capable of getting wide-spread appeal.

Of course, the reason campaigns are relatively cheap is they use so much volunteer help (free labor) and the actual form of solicitation is face-to-face (the most effective method of asking). This face-to-face method is called "peer solicitation." For many years, the only kind of "peer" that could ask someone for a gift was a "financial peer" (someone on the same economic level). The trouble with this system was that it encouraged "feather-bedding." One week Joe would ask Sam to give $1,000 to his favorite charity, then the next week Sam would ask Joe to contribute to his. This system has obvious limitations, so lately "peer" has come to mean "social peer." The executive director or the president of the board of directors of the charity may now call on the president of a company with hopes of getting a gift, without the fear that the president of the company will return the favor the following week.

Please be aware that capital funds campaigns are directed to getting capital funds (usually to build a building, add a wing, etc.) not for getting endowments funds or annual operating money. If used properly, a capital funds campaign will be required only once every ten or twenty years. (*Note*: This is becoming more and more untrue. Many organizations, especially universities, are starting capital campaigns that last ten years or more, and then they have only a brief rest before beginning another one! No one knows if this will continue to work for a long time.)

Until the 1960's, capital campaigns used to have goals of smaller amounts (the top campaigns were for \$10 or \$15 million). Lately, however, the goals have gone far higher, with a university recently announcing a goal of over \$300 million. It's obvious this can't go on forever, but it's also obvious that the top hasn't been reached yet.

Campaigns of this type also operate under the 80-20 rule. This means that 80 per cent of the gifts will come from 20 per cent of the donors. This is a guess, of course, for I have seen campaigns where 90 per cent of the money came from 3 per cent of the donors, and a case where 75 per cent of the money came from 25 per cent of the donors. But, in general, this means that you will get a small number of very large gifts. This has many consequences for you.

The basic one is that the best time to raise money is before the campaign is announced. And you must raise the money among the Board of Directors. A rule of thumb is that 15 per cent of the goal must come from this group. Another rule of thumb is that you must have at least three prospects for a 10 per cent gift (if the goal is \$150,000, a 10 per cent gift is \$15,000) for the campaign to be successful. Solicit the major gift prospects first, so when you announce the campaign, you're already significantly toward the goal. This generates enthusiasm and involvement from the 80 per cent of the people who will give the remaining 20 per cent of the money.

Because campaigns work on the principle of "peer solicitation," it is not uncommon to have a minimum of four hundred to six hundred people involved in a small campaign. Larger goals require larger numbers, with thousands of volunteers necessary for goals over \$1 million. You can determine the number of volunteers you need by dividing the number of prospects by five. This is the Rule of Fives: One person will call on five others.

Someone once said that organizing a campaign is a matter of breaking down a very major task into an infinite number of small tasks which can be done and done effectively by a large group of people. But this observation, while true, is not confined to campaigns. In a sense, all work of any type or size is done in that manner.

What are some more helpful guidelines?

Normally, you will be successful if your estimates of the amounts of money you want to ask for total 300 per cent or more of your goal. Another standard to judge your goal by is it should be three times the highest amount you've ever raised in one year. And within the goal, use the 1/3, 1/3, 1/3 approach. (See Campaign Organization #11, pg. 105) What you'll have then is a system of quotas telling you how much you must get from each level of giving in order to meet your goal. These quotas will, in turn, help the giver decide how much he will give. Part of the success of the campaign will be determined by how high you set your expectations. Set your quotas high, then urge each section to strive to meet its goal.

Am I hinting you should use *pressure* to get gifts in the campaign? Yes, definitely! The only way to reach a large goal is for everyone to feel a sense of immediacy, of urgency. Be sure that everyone realizes how important the task is that they're involved with. And keep telling them.

When should capital campaigns be held? Of course, this is not a problem with campaigns with large goals ($10 million and over), for they must go on all the time. But under that amount, there are some guidelines. Basically they say when you should not have a campaign: summer, Christmas, and when the United Way has its drive.

If all of this seems very simple, that's because it is. It is simple in theory, but difficult to carry out.

Before you begin, be sure to conduct a feasibility study

A capital funds campaign is such a complex task you should use every possible standard to decide if you should get into it. The main tool professional fund-raisers have in this situation is the feasibility study.

Before a fund-raiser will undertake a capital campaign he requires a contract with you to do the feasibility study. He too wants to be sure you should have the campaign.

Depending on the size of the campaign goal and whether the campaign will be nationwide, it will take between two weeks and several months and will cost from $1,000 to $100,000—or more.

Here are the questions from an actual feasibility study I use.

How to find out if you can raise the money you need

I. *Organization background.*

A. Organization and board of directors

1. When started?
2. Describe geographical area it serves.
3. Describe population of the service area.
4. Board of directors
   a.) How many on board of directors? Men? Women?
   b.) How many are businessmen?
      1) How many are in top management?
      2) How many are opinion-leaders in the community?
   c.) How many are *deeply* involved with the organization?
   d.) How many have well-above-average incomes?
   e.) How much have they contributed?
   f.) How well do the executive directors get along?
5. What are the major strengths of the staff as a whole? What are their major weaknesses?
6. Do the office facilities meet the needs of the staff? Of the program?

B. What services are offered by the organization?

1. Does it duplicate the services of any other community organization?
2. How do its services compare with those in other communities?
3. Does it cooperate with other organizations in joint programs?
4. How long have they operated?
5. How many people use these services?
6. Have they been added to or cut back? What are the reasons?
   a.) Has it received any complaints?
   b.) How does it handle complaints?
7. How much does each of your programs cost separately?
8. What is distinctive about your organization? Your programs?
9. How would you use an extra $1,000,000 if you receive it this year?

10. Do you have a written long-range plan for your organization?
11. How many volunteers do you have? Can you think of any methods for involving more people?
12. How do you measure the results of your program?
13. Is there a job you're not presently doing that you think you should do?

C. History of the organization
  1. What has been the growth rate of the service area?
  2. How many potential members or users of its service can you expect?

D. Annual operating budget
  1. What is the amount necessary?
  2. Who makes the major contributions?
  3. Are there any products or services sold that help raise money?
  4. Do they have a membership drive?
  5. Does the organization operate at a loss?
  6. What does the organization charge for its services?
     a.) Is it competitive?
  7. Have any private sources of funding been developed?
  8. Will it receive any wills and bequests?
  9. What are the assets and liabilities of the organization?

E. If you have decided that you want a campaign to raise money:
  1. What is your goal?
  2. Why do you want this money?
  3. Why is it *necessary* that you have this money?

F. Public relations
  1. What media use the announcements that are put out?
     a.) Radio, TV, or newspapers?
     b.) The announcements cover which events? What sort of things do they make announcements about?
  2. Internal public relations
     a.) Is there a newspaper?
     b.) A newsletter?
     c.) An annual report?
     d.) A recognition program for volunteers?

e.) A suggestion program so that you can get effective change in the organization?

3. General considerations
   a.) How much do you spend on public relations?
   b.) Is one person responsible?
   c.) Is it limited to reporting its actions or does it interpret its actions to the community?
   d.) Does it put out news releases; does it put out photographs along with the releases?
   e.) Does it go to other organizations for help?
   f.) When was the last time that it held an, "open house?" (This gives good publicity. Even if it is not well attended, it gets the organization's name before people.)
   g.) Is an attempt made to get some community leaders at its outstanding program events?

II. *Survey of community leaders.* This is an opinion survey with the names suggested by the organization. You should pick names of general community leaders, and you should interview twenty to thirty people. Be sure to include an appendix with important quotations by interviewees.

A. These are the questions you should ask:
   1. Is the organization well liked and generally well known?
   2. Do you feel well informed about its program?
   3. What do you think of their public relations? What needs immediate attention?
   4. How large is their service area?
   5. Does this area have a great deal of civic pride as an entity?
   6. What is the economic trend of the area?
   7. Has the community recently united to accomplish a specific goal?
   8. Have there been fund drives in the area lately?
   9. Why have they been successful? List campaigns in order of importance.
   10. Is the board of directors strong?
   11. Is the campaign necessary to raise the money for the purposes they have in mind?
   12. Do you think many other people feel the same way?
   13. Will industry in the area help?

14. How much could be raised in a well-conducted campaign?
15. Special contributions available? Is 10 per cent available somewhere?
16. Is good leadership available for campaign?
17. Who would you suggest for campaign chairman?
18. Are there factions in the community?
19. Are there factions over this organization?
20. Is the idea of professional fund-raiser disliked?
21. Is there a special season when attitudes toward a professional fund-raiser would be favorable?
22. What kind of support is available in the community?
23. Would you or your firm be willing to support the drive financially?
24. Would you personally be willing to help with time and effort?

III. *Service Area.* This section discusses statistical and economic data about a specific geographic area, with special notes about the major population areas.

A. Population and economic growth.

1. Comparative population sizes.
   a.) Population changes in the last few years.
   b.) Growth of major population centers in the service area.
   c.) Breakdown of whites and non-whites.
   d.) Movement of population. (Are they going to the suburbs; is there any movement within your area?)
   e.) Where are the wealthy areas?
   f.) Is there a predominant religion or nationality group? What per cent belong to them, how do they feel about your service or organization?
2. Are there any major prejudices in the community?
3. Average age of residents.
4. How do they spend their income?
   a.) *Sales Management* (magazine) every June publishes a Dept. of Commerce report which is a breakdown of the average income and expenditures for every county.
   b.) Number of families in your area.
   c.) What is their buying (disposable) income?

5. How does your area compare to others in the state? In the nation? Are you in a low, medium, or high market area?
6. Communications influence in the service area.
   a.) Circulation of newspapers.
   b.) How many television homes?
   c.) Where should you plant your best public relations?
7. What major industries are in the area?
   a.) Total manufacturing payroll.
   b.) What per cent is applicable to the major industries? (The Pacific Northwest, for example, is predominantly lumbering and aerospace; if they are not doing too well, then a capital funds campaign will not do too well.)
   c.) What is the strength of the major industries? What is the forecast? (Banks will often give you this information.)
8. Look at the total bank deposits in the area. Are they rising or falling?
9. Look at passenger and commercial auto sales and their trends.
10. Wholesale and retail sales and their trends.
11. Building construction.
    a.) What per cent owns their own home?
    b.) Apartments being built? (People that are permanent in the area take more interest in civic organizations than people who are transient.
12. Look at other campaigns in the area.
    a.) What were their goals for the last five years?
    b.) Have they attained their goals?
        1) If so, how have they done it?
        2) If not, why not? What were their problems? What are their strengths and what are their weaknesses?

IV. *The Negative and Positive Aspects.*

A. Negative Aspects. Typical problems include:

1. Small effective giving population.

2. Extremely negative comments from your twenty or thirty interviews.
3. Small chance of getting foundation grant.
4. Too many organizations in the area with duplicating services or programs.
5. A weak board.
6. A lack of awareness about the organization's programs.

B. Positive Aspects. Sometimes these factors outweigh the negative ones:

1. Tremendous spirit in the organization may make up for a a lot of faults in other areas.
2. An economic boom forecast for the major industries of the service area.
3. Now is the best time to conduct a campaign.
4. There is little competition for funds.
   a.) No other major drives are forecast.
5. There is tremendous community spirit in the area.
6. You can get support from businessmen.

V. *Conclusion and Recommendations.*

A. What is the goal of the campaign?

1. What are the monetary needs?
2. If you are going to hire a professional fund-raiser, what is his fee?
3. What are the probable expenses of the campaign?
4. What does that total?

B. Is the goal reasonable?

1. Use information from interviews. Can the money be raised?
2. What problems are expected in reaching the goal?
3. What positive aspects are there to the goal?
4. Where is intensive effort needed (usually public relations)?
5. Do the people in this area give away money?
6. Can the campaign succeed here?
   a.) If yes:
      1) What is the minimum need? What is potentially available (feasible)?
      2) Work out a program of service.

VI. *Appendix.*

A. Proposed budget outline.

B. Names of the people interviewed and their business and position.

C. Quotations of people interviewed.

Notes for a $150,000 Campaign: If you hire a professional fund-raiser, there is a man who comes in for a couple of weeks and builds prospect files; he paves the way, lines up volunteers, sets up an office, etc. He goes away for a month and lets the organization recuperate. Then the campaign director comes in for about four months. During this time only one month is used for raising money. Most of the time is used for adequate planning and public relations.

What are the three major reasons for capital campaign failures?

1. *The chairman.* He's the most important element in the campaign. If you don't get a good one, your campaign will fail. Why is this, when so many other people are involved? It's the 80-20 rule working. If most of your money comes from a few big gifts, it follows that someone capable of getting large amounts must solicit them. In most cases, this must be the chairman. So he should be both wealthy and influential. He must be accepted as an equal when he asks for large sums, and he should be able to give a large gift himself. Also he should be enthusiastic and committed and involved with the cause. How else could he enlist the support of other influential people?

2. *Not enough volunteers.* Too many organizations try to have capital campaigns when they are too young (say, under ten years). That's usually too soon because they don't have a large enough membership or large enough group of potential members. If you make that mistake, there won't be enough people to do the calling and there won't be enough people to call on! This difficulty is actually the opposite of the 80-20 rule. Since 20 per cent of the people are giving so much of the money, the rest of the people (80 per cent) must give the balance. If there aren't enough people, the balance won't come in, and the campaign will fall of its own weight. Be sure you have enough volunteers who will do the calling before you start a campaign.

3. *Not asking for enough money.* This points to a frequent difficulty in campaigns: There is a very high rate of failure in campaigns that have goals of less than $150,000. The rate of failure here is much higher than if the goal is greater than $150,000. However, you should be cautious. Don't just run out and increase your goal. That would also cause failure (unrealistic thinking). The moral is: If your goal is less than $150,000, be on the lookout for failure. Take extra precautions!

Campaign organization table of contents

1. *Organization Chart* (See page 109)

The campaign is organized in the pyramid style. One person gets five people to join; those five each get five (they get twenty-five altogether); each of those five get five more (125); and so on, until you have as many as you need. But how many will you need? A simple way is to count the total number of people you want to ask for gifts and divide that number by five. That will give you the number of workers you need.

The pyramid style of organization requires large numbers of workers.

Also, it's true that the more workers you have, the more money you'll raise. Most of your success will be determined by your ability to get other people involved in the campaign.

As do all organizations that have large numbers of workers, you'll have trouble getting people to actually do what they say they'll do. The very size of the bureaucracy makes it difficult for you to get the "supervisors" to follow up on their workers. You should expect only 10 to 20 per cent of the workers to finally make their calls and ask for the gifts.

2. *Budget* (See page 109)

The total budget for the campaign, as a rule of thumb, ought to be about 10 to 15 per cent of the goal. However, it's not figured on a percentage basis. A professional fund-raiser will charge on a fee basis for the number of man-hours worked. Office expenses, secretaries, paper, printing, supplies, postage, etc., are additional.

The total of these fees and expenses should be between 10 and 15 per cent. The larger the goal, the smaller the expenses will be as a percentage of that goal. So, in the capital campaign for $100,000 the costs may be $15,000 (15 per cent). In the capital campaign for $1,000,000, the costs may be $100,000 (10 per cent).

The professional fund-raiser will require a contract that agrees to pay him for the total amount of hours he spends on the campaign. This fee must be paid whether or not the full goal is reached, and you should know that it is unethical for a fund-raiser to accept his fee on a percentage of the total amount raised. Therefore, you should be sure to talk with the fund-raiser's past clients and, specifically, you should speak personally to the person on his staff who will be your campaign director.

3. *Campaign Calendar* (See page 110)

The larger the goal, the longer the campaign. For $100,000, it will take four to five months. For $250,000 it will take seven to eight months. For $1,000,000 it will take twelve to fourteen months.

The largest amount of time in the campaign will not be spent in asking people for money. That will be done in a relatively short period of time (about 40 per cent). Most of the rest of the time will be used to plan the campaign; to get the people who will do the asking; to take care of the printing; to write brochures; and to develop the films and slide presentations you will use. Preparation is the main task in the campaign. The better the preparation, the more money you'll raise.

4. *General Campaign Plan* (See page 115)

So everybody knows that everything is organized and that there are definite deadlines.

5. *Preliminary Service Campaign* (See page 118)

During this time, there is recruitment of key leadership, building the prospect file, and the preparation of campaign literature. Again, the better the preparation, the more money you'll raise.

6. *Responsibilities of the General Chairman* (See page 119)

If your general chairman gets a chance to read this, he'll wish he never agreed to help. A lot is expected of him, and if he fails, the campaign will fail. Be sure he knows that he's supposed to get people to be chairmen of specific committees and also to ask them for a gift (preferably a big one). If he can face up to these facts, then he'll probably do all right. But be sure he's informed of the scope of his responsibilities.

7. *Arrangements and Public Relations Committee* (See page 123)

The public relations committee should make sure your publicity releases are used by the radio stations, TV stations, and the newspapers. It's helpful if you can get people who are announcers, station managers, reporters, or editors to be on the committee.

Most campaigns have either slide presentation or a combination of slides and tape recordings. They can create tremendous impact by showing the emotional side of the appeal. In more elaborate campaigns, or where you have someone who has a special skill, it's good to have a full sound movie.

The campaign brochures and information sheets will be prepared by the professional fund-raiser who is campaign director. Also he makes the "arrangements" for any kick-off meeting or rally or large gathering of people during the campaign. The reason the arrangements and public relations committee should help with this is that they should be able to ask a friend to rent a meeting room as a favor and thereby lower the costs. This committee has no solicitation duties, but members of it are asked by their chairman to make individual gifts.

8. *Major Gift Prospects* (See page 126)

Ask everyone, "Do you know anyone you think might be a prospect for a major gift?" (A major gift prospect is someone who will contribute at least $1,000 over a three-year pledge period. Normally, this means he should have an annual income of at least $20,000.)

The most critical area of a capital campaign is the solicitation of major gifts. So it's very important to get as many names of major gift prospects as possible. Rack your brains. Look in the city directory. Look in the newspaper. Look in your own membership. (Anyone who has ever given $100 or more should be a prospect.) At this stage, you should not worry about whether they'll actually make a gift—just whether they have the capacity to make a gift.

9. *Progress Review and Audit Committee* (See page 128)

This committee should be made up of bankers, lawyers and accountants—and anyone else you think knows the financial position of many of the people you will solicit. The people on this committee should decide how much to ask each prospect for (another critical area). Even here, however, the emphasis should be on how much the prospect is capable of giving, not whether you will actually be successful in getting that amount.

10. *"Answers to Questions Most Frequently Asked"* (See page 131)

This is the one brochure that should be in all campaigns. It is in question and answer form and the questions are very basic ones. You'd be surprised how many people can't think of the answers to many simple questions about the charity when they're speaking to a prospect. This brochure helps in that situation.

11. *Gift-Investment Analysis* (See page 135)

It's been documented in thousands of campaigns: about one third of the money will come from the top ten gifts, another third from the next one hundred gifts, and the last third from all the other gifts. This "Gift-Investment Analysis" tells you what quotas to set in a $150,000 campaign.

12. *Memorial Gift-Investment Opportunities* (See page 136)

No campaign should be without memorial gift opportunities. When people get to the stage of making a major contribution, they frequently want to buy immortality with the gift. Be sure to have a list of possible memorials ready, and be sure to include this information in all major gift presentations.

One interesting feature of memorial gifts is they frequently encourage giving in a larger amount than the prospect first had in mind. There is more prestige connected with a more expensive item than a cheap one.

13. *Major Individuals Section Chart of Organization* (See page 137)

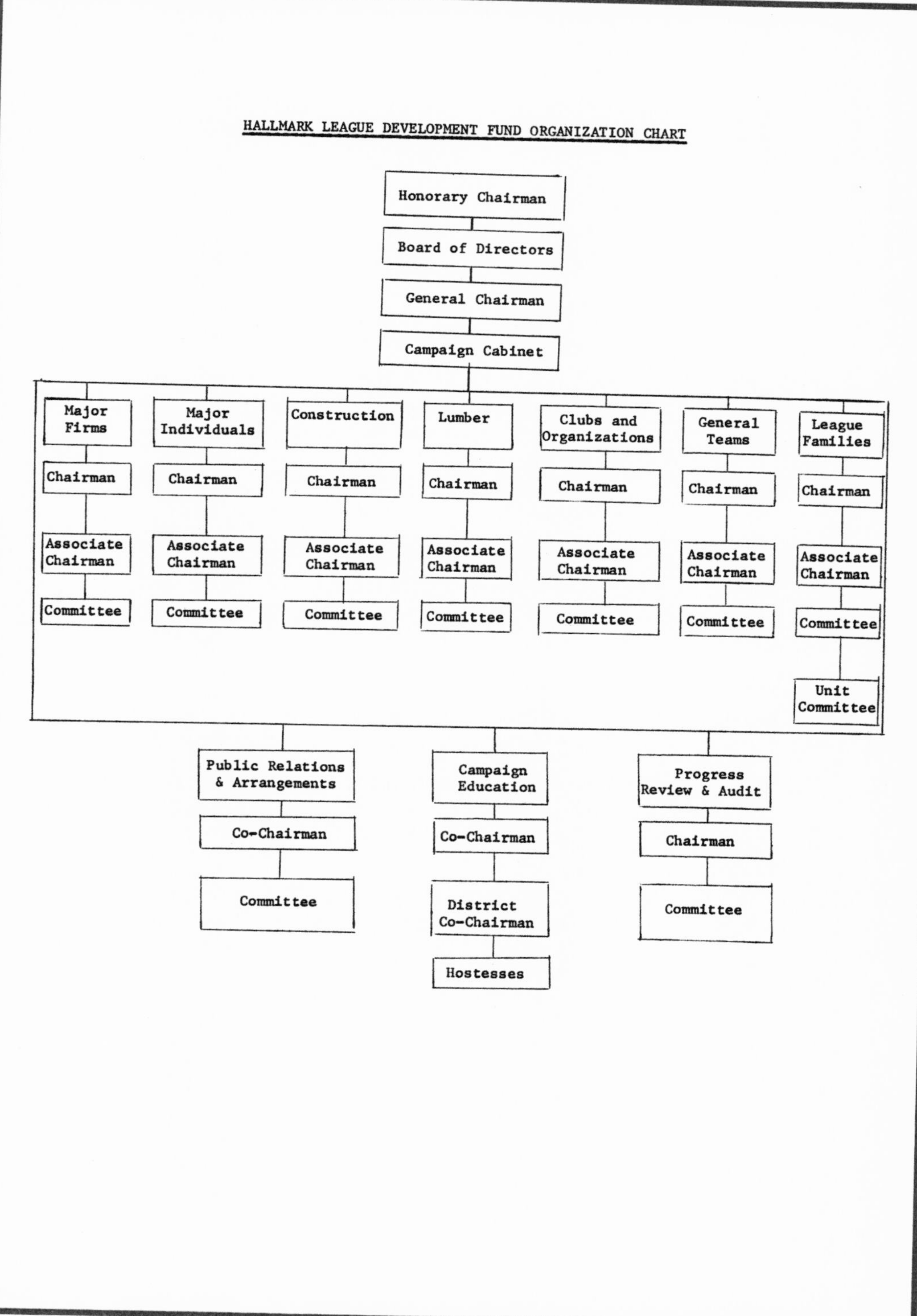
HALLMARK LEAGUE DEVELOPMENT FUND ORGANIZATION CHART
Honorary Chairman
Board of Directors
General Chairman
Campaign Cabinet
Major Firms
Chairman
Associate Chairman
Committee
Major Individuals
Chairman
Associate Chairman
Committee
Construction
Chairman
Associate Chairman
Committee
Lumber
Chairman
Associate Chairman
Committee
Clubs and Organizations
Chairman
Associate Chairman
Committee
General Teams
Chairman
Associate Chairman
Committee
League Families
Chairman
Associate Chairman
Committee
Unit Committee
Public Relations & Arrangements
Co-Chairman
Committee
Campaign Education
Co-Chairman
District Co-Chairman
Hostesses
Progress Review & Audit
Chairman
Committee

14. *Major Individuals Section Chart of Organization* (See page 137)

15. *Major Individuals Section Calendar* (See page 138)

16. *Major Individuals Section Campaign Plan* (See page 139)

17. *Major Individuals Section Kick-Off Meeting Agenda* (See page 144)

These five pieces are detailed break-downs of one section of the campaign, the Major Individuals Section. All the other sections should be detailed in a similar manner. These details should be given to each member of the committee, so they realize where they fit in.

18. *"Away We Go!"* (See page 145)

A note of encouragement to all the solicitors in the campaign, which is given to them at the Kick-Off meeting.

Estimated Campaign Expense Budget

Secretarial assistance (5 months)	$3,500
Office and equipment rental	1,200
Printing and postage	3,050
Telephone and telegraph	250
Office supplies	500
Travel, meeting expenses and miscellaneous	1,000
Total	$9,500

Schedule of Deadlines and Events

February	10	Open campaign office and hire office staff
	14	Finalize campaign plan and duties of general chairman
	17	Prepare printed material and audio-visual aids
	22	Deadline for enlistment of soliciting and non-soliciting leadership
	24	Campaign cabinet meeting
	25	Clubs and organization meeting
	26	Arrangements and public relations meeting
	27	Progress review and audit meeting
	28	Deadline for enlistment of major firms, major individuals, lumber and construction association chairmen
March	3	Campaign cabinet meeting
	4	Major firms, major individuals, construction & lumber association chairmen organization meeting
	5	Deadline for enlistment of clubs & organization association chairmen

6 deadline for enlistment of campaign education district co-chairwomen
7 Deadline for enlistment of league families chairmen
10 Campaign cabinet meeting
12 League families district chairmen organization meeting
17 Campaign cabinet meeting
18 Campaign education district co-chairwomen organization meeting
19 Clubs and organization associate chairmen meeting
21 Deadline for enlistment of major gifts, construction and lumber committee members
24 Campaign cabinet meeting
25 Deadline for enlistment of clubs & organizations committee members
26 Major gifts, construction, and lumber kick-off meeting
27 Deadline for enlistment of league families section chairmen
28 Deadline for enlistment of general teams association chairmen
31 Campaign cabinet meeting

April 1 Major firms and major industries first report
2 Construction and lumber first report
3 General teams team captains' organization meeting
4 Deadline for enlistment of campaign education hostesses
7 Campaign cabinet meeting
8 Major firms and major industries second report
9 Construction and lumber second report
10 League families section chairmen organization meeting
11 Deadline for enlistment of general teams committee members
14 Campaign cabinet meeting
15 Major firms and major industries third report
16 Construction and lumber third report
17 Deadline for enlistment of league families section committee members
18 Campaign education hostesses organization meeting
21 Campaign cabinet meeting
22 Major firms, major industries, construction, and lumber fourth report

	24	General teams and league families kick-off
	28	Campaign cabinet meeting
	29	First general report
May	5	Campaign cabinet meeting
	6	Second general report
	12	Campaign cabinet meeting
	13	Third general report
	19	Final report meeting
	21	Campaign report to executive board
	22	Close office

Hallmark League Development Fund

Campaign Headquarters

#1 Nor Street

Telephone

342-4993

General Campaign Plan

Program Purposes:

(1) To create a cohesive, enthusiastic sales force essential to the achievement of the Campaign Minimum Need.

(2) To raise the Minimum Campaign Need so that development of the improved retreat may be started.

(3) To conduct an intensive, comprehensive, and stimulating educational program that will establish a sound foundation for future Hallmark League growth.

Campaign Dates:............February 15 thru May 15

Minimum Need of the Program:..........is $150,000.00 so that it will be possible to proceed with the proposed improvement program at the retreat.

Prospective Gift-Investors:..........To be called upon include businesses, industries, clubs and organizations, and individuals throughout the council who either have or should have an interest in this important community endeavor and are in a position to support it financially.

Memorial Opportunities:..........will be available to those seeking to perpetuate their name, a loved one or a business firm. Recognition of such memorial gift-investments will be made by inserting the name of the gift-investor and that in honor of whom the gift-investment is made on plaques, to be located in such a place and manner as are consonant with the nature of the memorial unit.

Payment Period:..........will commence at the time the gift-investment is made or at the election of the gift-investor.

Organization Procedure:..........dynamic civic leadership will guide and coordinate active, responsible, committee built on echlon structure. Manpower will be utilized in such a manner as to reduce the work load of any individual and to produce the most effective functioning units.

Success:..........depends in great measures on building unified, forceful committees which, if blended with early pace-setting gift-investments, will provide impact, confidence, and inspiration.

Hallmark League

Development Campaign

To: Julian Hamilton

From: Thompson White

Re: Summary Outline of Preliminary Service

October 28 - November 8

1. Building of Prospect File for Civic Section

   A. This file includes hundreds of Prospect Master Cards, which indicate names of company (or club, etc.), address, and name and phone number of contact (if shown).

   B. This file was compiled primarily from information furnished by most of the Chamber of Commerce offices in the council service area. However, no replies were received from some areas as of this date.

   C. This file will be organized into the following five sub-sections of the overall civic section:

      1) Major firms

      2) Major individuals

      3) General business

      4) Clubs and organizations, including foundations

      5) Construction companies

   D. Evaluation will take place between February 15 and March 30.

2. Recruitment of Key Leadership

   A. Not much progress was made as far as actual recruiting of key volunteer leadership for the campaign.

   B. Ken has not decided yet whether he will be able or willing to serve as council president during 1969.

C. Selection of a campaign General Chairman was discussed briefly on three or four occasions. Dean and Joe seemed to be the preferred choices. Other men mentioned included Ted, Ehrman, Dick, Hale Thompson, Wyatt Lambert, and John. Discussion concerned Civic Chairman and League Family Chairman, as well as General Chairman.

D. Prospective Leadership Master Cards have been filled out for all members of the Board of Directors and many other friends of the Hallmark League (list prepared by Julian Hamilton).

3. Preparation of Campaign Literature

A. The following items have been completed:

(A.K. Company is our printer and Ed is our contact)

1) Question and answer leaflet (proof completed)

2) League Family leaflet (Ed working on proof)

3) Memorial leaflet (Ed working on proof)

4) Information booklet (draft completed)

5) Regular mailing envelope (proof completed)

6) Salesman's report envelope (proof completed)

7) Pledge card (Proof completed)

4,000 pledge cards will be delivered the week of November 18th.

B. Stencils can be prepared on the following information sheets:

1) List of news media

2) Fundamentals of successful campaigning

3) General campaign plan

4) General facts on campaign

5) Projected-gift investment chart

C. Other literature not needed until late in the campaign and the slide presentation will be prepared in February.

D. We need a campaign slogan. Opinion is best suggestions have been, "You can build a better tomorrow" and, "Help them through the magic years".

4. Other Matters

A. Approval has been received from the United Crusade Board of Uor City.

B. With the help of Ken and Bill, campaign office space has been secured in the Tiffany Building, probably rent free.

C. It will help if pledge cards are typed with necessary information (Mr. and Mrs., address, and area), and organized by area and group.

D. I met Mrs. Snively at Saks and informed her of the campaign and of help we would appreciate during it.

E. Just a thought - most of Henry's associates prefer to take the responsibility of hiring their own campaign secretary.

F. A tentative time schedule for the duration of the campaign will be prepared in February.

Development Campaign

The Retreat Development Campaign is scheduled to be conducted from February 15th through May 15th. The minimum need has been set at $150,000 over a three-year pledge period, in order to proceed with improvement of the primitive retreat.

Preliminary Service Phase

October 28 - November 8

1. Building of card file of all potential prospects.
   - A. League Family section
   - B. Civic section
     - 1) Major firms
     - 2) Major individuals
     - 3) General business
     - 4) Clubs and organizations, including foundations
     - 5) Construction companies
   - C. All prospects will be evaluated in February.
2. Recruiting of key volunteer campaign leadership. (see hand-out of skeleton organization chart.)
3. Preparing of campaign literature (A.K. Company will do our printing).
   - A. Pledge cards
   - B. Question and answer leaflet
   - C. League family leaflet
   - D. Memorial leaflet

Memo on the Responsibilities of the General Chairman

It is our fundamental purpose in this brief memorandum to outline the enlistment and solicitation responsibilities of the General Chairman. Where indicated, a few observations will be made as to the qualifications to be sought in those to be selected.

I need not tell you, I am certain, that we are embarking on a campaign that is most important to the Council and to the community and that many will say we cannot be successful. You are aware, of course, that there are many prophets of doom and that a negative attitude never produced anything but failure. If all worthwhile programs were entered into with that kind of spirit, human progress would be impossible.

At the very outset, it should be noted that leadership of every Section and Division must be first rate if victory is to be achieved. It must lead in word, action and giving. "The speed of the boss is the speed of the gang."

It should be in the mold of qualifications which singled you out as General Chairman:

. . . Strong convictions about worthwhile community programs.

. . . The ability to organize, lead, and inspire men.

. . . The ability to work harmoniously with key leaders.

. . . The willingness to make a sacrificial gift investment commensurate with individual means.

A. Enlistment Duties

1. Campaign Cabinet...should consist of the members of the Council's Board of Directors, together with all Campaign Section Chairmen. Deadline for Recruitment of Cabinet should be February 10.

2. Major Firms Section Chairman...to supervise the solicitation of the principal corporations and foundations; the chairman will enlist the Associate Chairmen; he will coordinate and supervise the work of his Associate Chairmen and will be responsible for securing gift investments from the Associate Chairmen he recruited.
3. Major Individuals Section Chairman...to secure gift investments from significant individual contributors in the community; the chairman will enlist the Associate Chairmen; he will coordinate and supervise the work of his Associate Chairmen and will be responsible for securing gift investments from the Associate Chairmen he recruited.
4. Construction Committee Chairman...who has contacts essential for securing gift investments in kind or services from those who might otherwise not be able or inclined to participate on a significant level.
5. Clubs and Organizations Section Chairman...to solicit those clubs and organizations in the community which might have the possibility of making a treasury gift to the campaign.
6. League Families Section Chairman...who, working with the professional staff, will conduct the solicitation among League Families.
7. Lumber Industry Chairman...who, along with the committee, will solicit the firms in this key industry.
8. General Teams Section Chairman...to solicit those prospects who should be contacted but who are not being solicited by other sections. This is the final solicitation phase of the program.
9. Public Relations Chairman...who will strategize in cooperation with the Campaign Director the general public information phase of the appeal and will counsel in the preparation of all campaign visual aids as well as assisting in the planning of informative materials.

10. Progress Review and Audit Committee Chairman...who will assist, with a committee of ten (10), in the building and analysis of the Master Prospect File

11. Campaign Education Co-Chairwomen...two women who will organize a massive Women's Educational Committee which will endeavor to bring the message to every potential home, will assist through a telephone crusade to assure a massive attendance at the General Inaugural, and to again, assure, as a result of the telephone crusade, that gift investors in the General Teams Section are aware of the fact that they will be called upon to participate in this challenging appeal.

B. Solicitation Duties

1. To solicit, with the assistance of the Executive Director and the Campaign Cabinet.

2. To solicit: Major Firms Chairman; Major Individuals Section Chairman; Construction Committee Chairman; Clubs and Organizations Section Chairman; League Families Section Chairman; Lumber Industry Chairman; General Teams Section Chairman; Public Relations Chairman; Progress Review and Audit Committee Chairman; Campaign Education Committee Co-Chairwomen.

A Final Word

There is no escaping the simple fact that the General Chairman, by word and example, sets the pace of the campaign. Your adherence to enlistment, recruitment, and solicitation deadlines will serve as an example for the Total Campaign Organization. To put it differently,

YOU ARE THE WAY!!

As a personal note, I am honored to be accorded the privilege of working with you in this - the most important appeal ever undertaken by the Hallmark League. We pledge you our untiring efforts in its fulfillment.

HPH:jvt

Hallmark League Development Fund

Campaign Headquarters

#1 Uor Street

Telephone

342-4993

Arrangements and Public Relations

It is the responsibility of the Arrangements and Public Relations Committee to plan the major meetings of the Campaign and to work with the Campaign Director in the preparation of printed and audio-visual materials and materials for release to the communications media.

Is Public Relations Necessary?

Every organization has public relations. There is no choice as to whether to "take public relations or omit it." The choice is between good public relations and bad public relations.

What Do We Mean by Public Relations?

Definitions of public relations vary widely. However, we are limiting this presentation to public relations as an aid to fund-raising. First, public relations in modern fund-raising is based upon performance. Whereas, announcements will be made concerning future events, credit for achievement will be taken only after "performance". Good public relations is not based on press agentry, stunts, gimmicks, or high pressure promotion. In some instances, the public relations program can actually achieve more by promising less than will actually be achieved.

People are always pleased to see results in excess of projections, and they are distrubed by results which are less than were promised.

Good public relations techniques are the means of reflecting, outside the organization, the good performance achieved inside.

<u>Where Good Public Relations Takes Us</u>

If it is accepted that good public relations has its foundations in good performance, then surely there is an extraordinary opportunity for positive results in the Hallmark League Retreat Development Fund where day-to-day functions are characterized by "service to people".

The recommendations which are made here should be considered as a check list -- as an outline which the campaign can utilize and tailor to its own character; relate to the Retreat Development Fund, and later, adapt to regular League public relations.

<u>Public Relations Program for the Growth-in-Action Fund</u>

The Public Relations Committee will use all possible publicity and public relations media available to the program in preparing and presenting timely and educationally informative material. All public releases to the news media will have a release date which, if followed, will facilitate timely newspaper and radio coverage.

<u>Media and Visuals</u>

Newspaper and radio, Major Brochure, Question-Answer Pamphlet, 35m.m. color slide -- sound presentation, and personal letters.

It should be noted that the maximum value of the public relations program will be realized only as the public is made aware of the total program and the specific publics (Business, Industry Chambers of Commerce, Substantial Individuals, Educators, Service Clubs, etc.) are made aware of their opportunity for living gift-investments. No single public relations contact can be assumed to "do the job". The final result will be achieved by <u>full</u> exposure to the <u>total</u> program.

Media Release Time Schedule

March 2	Honorary Chairman and General Chairman Announcement.
March 3	Major Firms Chairman Announcement.
March 6	Major Individuals Chairman Announcement.
March 9	Lumber and Construction Chairmen Announcement.
March 12	General Teams Chairman Announcement.
March 14	Clubs and Organizations Chairman, Campaign Education Co-Chairwomen, Public Relations and Arrangements Chairman, Progress Review and Audit Chairman, General Announcement Picture of all Chairmen together and Caption.
March 16	Retreat Proposed Development.
March 26	Major Gifts Kick-Off Announcement.
April 1	Major Gifts Report Announcement.
April 2	Construction and Lumber Report Announcement.
April 15	Major Gifts and Lumber and Construction Report Announcement.
April 20	The League Feature Story.
April 22	Major Gifts and Construction and Lumber Report Announcement.
April 23	General Teams Mailing Announcement.
April 24	General Teams Kick-Off Announcement.
	Pass-Out-Buttons to Shoppers Story.
April 29	First General Report Meeting Announcement.
May 6	Second General Report Meeting Announcement.
May 13	Third General Report Meeting Announcement.
May 19	Final Report Meeting Announcement.

Hallmark League Development Fund

<u>Campaign Headquarters</u>   <u>Telephone</u>

#1 Uor Street   342-4993

An Important Memorandum

To: All Section Chairmen

From: Wyatt Lambert, IV, General Campaign Chairman

Re: Prospective Significant Individual Gift-Investors

- -

In the process of building the Prospect File for our Retreat Development Fund, we have a challenge which could lay a solid fund-raising foundation if it is met with resourcefulness. That is, the listing of individuals who can make significant gift-investments to the appeal . . . if they are <u>properly</u> <u>approached</u> and <u>called</u> <u>upon</u>. We have no problem securing the names of businesses and foundations, but we do have a real problem obtaining the names of substantial individuals (including widows and maiden ladies) who should be in our Major Individuals Prospect File.

As a consequence, we ask you to search your memory for the names and addresses of <u>Individuals</u> who could be significant gift-investors to the Development Fund. Whatever additional data you can provide about each person will be most helpful.

For the sake of the campaign, we ask you to complete your lists and bring them with you to the Cabinet Meeting on March 18.

All completed forms should be returned no later than March 18. The thought and care you exercise in the preparation of your individual list may well spell the difference between a "we almost made it" and a successful appeal for the Development Fund. While some of the names you suggest may be duplicated on other lists, be assured that all lists submitted will be tabulated and duplications eliminated. Above all, the information you submit will be held in the strictest confidence and the source will never be revealed.

If you have any questions, please contact Campaign Headquarters; the number is 342-4993.

General Instructions

1. List the names of individuals of financial ability who, in your judgment, may have an interest in the Development Fund or whose interest can be cultivated. Make your lest as comprehensive as possible. Additional forms can be obtained from Campaign Headquarters. We are only interested in the names of individuals at this time.
2. In Column 3, indicate generally the person's ability to make a gift-investment.
   A. $25,000 or more
   B. $10,000 or more
   C. $1,000 to $10,000
   D. $1,000 to $5,000
3. In Column 4, indicate who the proper person might be to make the personal contact.

Hallmark League Development Fund

Campaign Headquarters | Telephone
#1 Uor Street | 342-4993

To: Progress Review and Audit Committee

From: Daniel Fritz, Campaign Director

Subject: Progress Review Instructions

- -

The success of any campaign for funds is determined by the prospect file. If this file is to be an effective fund-raising device, it must be objectively evaluated.

The Progress Review Committe is, therefore, one of the most important active committees. The membership of this committee must be anonymous because of the confidential nature of the information with which it must deal.

Nine Fundamental Considerations

1. The goal for Hallmark League Retreat Development Fund is a minimum of $150,000.
2. This is a Capital Fund Drive as contrasted to a simple Fund-Raising Campaign.
3. We shall discard any figures of gifts to other projects except as such gifts will establish very general categories of civic interest and competence.
4. We shall direct our effort in an honest endeavor to arrive at the "suggested support amount" for each prospective gift-investor.

5. A "suggested support amount" is an evaluation of what the gift-investor's <u>fair</u> share of the objective should be, eliminating guesswork insofar as possible, according to the best informed judgment of the Committee members. No prospect should be evaluated on the basis of his willingness to give. Often, the observation is made "'X' Prospect could easily give $5,000, but you will be lucky to get $500." The Prospect should be evaluated on the basis of what could be given if properly cultivated. Very seldom is more received than is requested. Unless we ask, we shall not receive.
6. Good judgment coupled with general knowledge of the financial ability of firms and individuals to give must govern the efforts of the Committee.
7. Investments in the "Retreat Development Fund" may be spread over a three year period.
8. This Capital Fund Appeal is a once-in-a-lifetime opportunity to make a gift-investment.

Our Guide

We shall take our prospects by various classifications and arrive at a reasonable standard which would be applied to one or two prospects in each classification and then measure the others accordingly. Our Prospective Gift-Investment Analysis Chart is the base of the evaluation procedure. Willingness and financial competence are to be taken into consideration in establishing goals for individuals or corporations.

A. Corporate

The quality of the Corporate Gift must be influenced by qualitative factors if our yardstick is to be fair. Among those factors less susceptible of actual measurement that must be considered in arriving at that share are:

1. The stature of the corporation in the community.
2. Its tradition of leadership.
3. The civic zeal of its executives.
4. Its earning power and net assets.
5. The concern of the corporation for the health of its employees and their families.
6. Its desire to carry its fair share of the total lead.

B. Individuals

Five factors suggest themselves as guides for evaluating individual gift-investors:

1. An individual's net assets or capital accumulation N.B. Without considering accumulated capital, an individual with an income of $15,000, if properly cultivated, should be considered as a prospective ($1,000 or more) gift-investor over a three year period. This amounts to just slightly more than two per cent (2%) of gross per annum.
2. A person's annual income.
3. Identifiable interests in this endeavor - its current objectives, and its long range benefits.
4. A person's sense of civic responsibility.
5. Record of giving to civic projects.

Hallmark League Development Fund

Campaign Headquarters

#1 Uor Street

Telephone

342-4993

"Answers to Questions Most Frequently Asked"

1. What is the Retreat Development Campaign?

   It is an area-wide and league-wide solicitation to provide needed improved facilities for the Hallmark League Retreat.

2. What is the Minimum Need?

   A minimum need of $150,000 has been determined to effect the master development plan for the retreat.

3. Why is the Program Necessary?

   The present retreat has been operating on a temporary basis for the past four years. The retreat is inadequate to properly serve our members, only 16% of whom attended the retreat last year. Both vast improvement and expansion to year-round usage are necessary to appeal to and benefit members and other interested parties.

4. Where is the Retreat Located?

   The one hundred and forty acre retreat is located just sixteen miles west of Uor City

5. Who Will Operate the Improved Retreat?

   The retreat will continue to be operated by the Hallmark League.

6. What Planning Went into This Project?

   The Blue Ribbon Committee of the Board of Directors has studied recreational needs of the League for the past ten years. The master plan is designed not only to meet current needs, but also those years to come.

7. <u>Does Our Appeal Have the Necessary Approval</u>?

Yes, approval has been gained from the United Crusade of Uor City.

8. <u>Does the United Crusade Provide Funds for Capital Improvement</u>?

No. United Crusade provides no money for retreat development.

9. <u>How Will the Money Be Raised</u>?

Through an area-wide and league-wide solicitation of industries, businesses, organizations, and selected individuals. The solicitation will be conducted by local volunteer committees.

10. <u>What Advantages Does the Retreat Offer</u>?

The retreat offers a unique program for league members and others too.

11. <u>Who May Attend the Retreat</u>?

Any league member in good standing or friends of league members in good standing, upon payment of proper fees.

12. <u>How Many Members Does the Hallmark League Have</u>?

The League Register shows a total of 1,260 members. Over the past thirty-one years, there has been no increase in memberships.

13. <u>How Many Members Went to the Retreat Last Year</u>?

Last year one hundred and seventy-eight members participated in the resident tennis program while one hundred and twenty-six members took advantage of summer riding school.

14. <u>Didn't the Council Conduct a Retreat Development Fund Drive Recently</u>?

No. In their eighteen years, the Hallmark League has never asked the general public for funds.

15. <u>How Will Funds Raised in the Campaign Be Used</u>?

According to a master plan, approved by the Board of Directors in consultation with the architectural and engineering firm of best consultants of Uor City.

16. How Can League Families Participate in the Campaign?

By helping to establish unit memorials that will not only help improve the retreat, but will, in addition, permanently honor the Hallmark League.

17. Are Individual and Personal Gift-Investments Available?

Yes.

18. How Will Living Gift Investments Be Recognized?

Each living gift-investment will be appropriately designed in a suitable place by a gold plaque on which will be inscribed the name of the investor or individual in whose honor the investment is made.

19. Are There Other Memorials Available?

Yes. Many parts of the retreat may be memorialized in honor of yourself, a business, a loved one or a friend.

20. How May I Pay My Gift-Investment?

Gift-investments may be paid annually, semi-annually, quarterly, or even monthly over a three-year period, in cash or as you desire.

21. May I Give Stocks or Real Estate?

Yes. If they have appreciated in value, there is a dual tax deduction. You may deduct the present market value from your income tax, and you avoid paying a capital gains tax.

22. Can Gifts in Kind Be Pledged to the Retreat?

Yes, gifts in kind such as lumber, building and road materials, labor and other services, are welcome. These gifts also have double tax advantages.

23. Are Gifts Tax-Deductible?

Yes, subject to maximum tax deductions allowed individuals or corporations, by the Internal Revenue Service.

24. <u>How Much Shall I Give?</u>

This is a matter for you to decide. We suggest you consider the urgent need for improved retreat facilities. Then, plan your gift over the thirty-six month pledge period.

25. <u>How Do I Make Out My Check?</u>

To the Hallmark League Retreat Development Fund.

Hallmark League

Development Fund

Prospective Gift - Investment Analysis

Gift Investment Range	No. of Gift-Investments	Cumulative Gift Investments	Total	Cumulative Total
$50,000 or more	1	1	$25,000	$25,000
$25,000 to $49,999	1	2	12,500	37,500
$10,000 to $24,999	5	7	25,000	62,500
$ 5,000 to $9,999	10	17	25,000	87,500
$ 2,500 to $4,999	20	37	25,000	112,500
$ 1,000 to $2,499	35	72	17,500	130,000
$ 500 to $999	50	122	12,500	142,500
$ 250 to $499	100	222	12,500	155,000
$ 100 to $249	250	472	12,500	335,000
$ 99 or under	1000	1,472	37,500	410,000

Memorial Gift-Investment Opportunities

Swimming Pool & Dressing Room	$45,000	1
Kitchen & Dining Hall Equipment	13,000	1
Chairman's Lodge - Retreat	12,000	1
CIT Cabin	11,000	1
Health Cabin	9,000	1
Director's Cabin	4,000	1
Cook's Cabin	5,000	1
Library-Nature Building	4,000	1
Camp Entrance Gate	1,500	1
Foot Bridge	2,000	1
Shooting Area (Skeet)	2,500	1
Archery Range	2,200	1
Truck	4,000	1
Vehicle Storage Shelter	2,500	1
Picnic Area	1,500	1
Canoes and Row Boats	300	12
Tents	250	2

Hallmark League Development Fund

Campaign Headquarters

#1 Uor Street

Telephone

342-4993

Major Individuals Section Chart of Organization

Major Individuals Chairman

Duties: To enlist four (4) Associate Chairmen to assist them; to coordinate and supervise the work of this Section; to be responsible for securing gift-investments of the four (4) Associate Chairmen; to contact some key potential gift-investors.

Major Individual Associate Chairman

Duties: To enlist three (3) Committee Members; to coordinate the work of those he has recruited; to be responsible for securing the gift-investments of his Committee Members; and to contact potential gift-investors in his Section.

Major Individuals Committee Members

Duties: Working in pairs, if possible, to personally contact the prospective gift-investors in this Section. To attend orientation and training meetings, and be present at Report Meetings.

Note: All leadership of the Major Individuals Section will be asked to make personal calls upon prospects in this Section

Hallmark League Development Fund

Campaign Headquarters — #1 Uor Street

Telephone — 342-4993

Major Individuals Calendar

Day	Date	Event
Friday	February 28	Deadline for Enlistment of Associate Chairman
Tuesday	March 4	Associate Chairman's Organization Meeting
Friday	March 21	Deadline for Enlistment of Committee Members
Wednesday	March 26	Section Kick-Off
Tuesday	April 1	First Report
Tuesday	April 8	Second Report
Tuesday	April 15	Third Report
Tuesday	April 22	Fourth Report

Hallmark League Development Fund

Campaign Headquarters

#1 Uor Street

Telephone

342-4993

Major Individuals Campaign Plan

General Purposes

1. To create a cohesive, enthusiastic sales force essential to the achievement of the campaign Minimum Need.
2. To raise the Minimum Campaign Need so the Hallmark League can build a greatly improved retreat.
3. To conduct an intensive, comprehensive, and stimulating educational program that will establish a sound foundation for future League growth.

Specific Purpose

1. To secure from key individuals in the League's service area significant gift-investments of from $1,000 and up as to provide the campaign with a success impetus.
2. To accept a specific section minimum objective.

Campaign Dates

February 15 to May 15.

Gift-Investments

Will be payable over a three year period (or four tax years) at the election of the gift-investor and may be made in cash, real estate, stocks or bonds.

Memorial Opportunities

Will be available to those seeking to perpetuate their name, a loved one, or a business firm. Recognition of such memorial gift-investments will be made by inserting the name of the gift investor or that in honor of whom the gift-investment is made on a plaque to be located in such a place and manner as is consonant with the nature of the memorial gift.

Payment Period

Will commence at the time the gift-investment is made or at the election of the gift-investor.

Organization Procedure

Is clearly outlined in the Major Individuals Section Chart of Organization which is a part of this presentation.

Giving Evaluations

Are essential for providing committee members and the prospective gift-investor with helpful guides. They will be determined by a Progress Review and Audit Committee. The "Ability to Give" is a determining factor.

Meetings

Are the only process of orienting and coordinating committee. Prompt and full attendance at all meetings is imperative.

Solicitation

Will be conducted in phases.

Subscribing Before Soliciting

Is a fund-raising principle utilized in this campaign. Each committee member will be asked to make his own gift-investment before calling on anyone else.

Success

Depends on the degree to which the Major Individuals Section is able to inspire a high level of gift-investment response from those who possess the ability to give in substantial measure.

118

Hallmark League Development Fund

Campaign Headquarters

#1 Uor Street

Telephone

342-4993

Major Individuals Section

Chairman's Enlistment Roster

Chairman's Name ______________________________

Address ______________________________ Telephone __________

A. Please enlist by Friday, February 28, four (4) individuals to serve as your Associate Chairmen.

Qualifications for Associate Chairmen:

1. Should have strong convictions about the importance of this appeal.
2. Should have the ability to organize, lead and inspire men.
3. Should have the ability to make a significant Gift-Investment.

Duties of Associate Chairmen:

1. To attend orientation and training meetings.
2. To recruit three Committee Members.
3. To personally contact three to five prospective gift-investors.
4. To attend all report meetings.

B. Bring or make certain that your Associate Chairmen attend with you at the Associate Chairmen's Orientation meeting of Tuesday, March 4.

C. By Friday, February 28, please forward one copy of this enlightment roster to Campaign Headquarters in the enclosed self-addressed envelope. Keep the other copy for your own records.

Associate Chairman's Name	Address	Telephone
1.		
2.		
3.		
4.		

Major Individuals Section

Kick-Off Meeting Agenda

Friday, May 9

7:30	Breakfast	All
8:00	Welcome	George R. Smathers
8:01	Introduction of Section Chairmen	Wyatt Lambert, IV
8:03	Introduction of Major Individuals Section Committee Members	Julian Hamilton
8:05	The Need for Development of Camp Wilani	Julian Hamilton
8:10	Slide Presentation	Daniel Fritz
8:20	Explanation of Kits	Daniel Fritz
8:25	Assigning of Prospect Cards	George R. Smathers
8:29	Closing	George R. Smathers

Hallmark League Development Fund

Campaign Headquarters

#1 Uor Street

Telephone

342-4993

Away We Go!

..... some thoughts that may be helpful to you in conducting your Major Individuals Section solicitation

These are important days that lie ahead for each of us. We have accepted an awesome responsibility. The success of the campaign weighs heavily upon our shoulders. This is not fancy! This is fact.

Between now and our First Report Meeting ... Friday, May 16 ... it is up to each of us individually to see to it that the prospects assigned us are called upon and that we adhere as closely as possible to our instructions.

(1) Sell the Campaign. The first offer may not be sufficient. It may be necessary to make a second call. But do not leave the Gift-Investment card. Keep it in your pocket until the prospect is ready to sign. It is your passport to return.

(2) Have as many of your calls made as possible ... at least the first time ... for the First Report Meeting. Make it a point to be at that First Report Meeting and to bring the signed cards with you. Only signed cards in hand can be recorded on the report board.

(3) Promote Memorials. A unique appeal challenges giving imaginations. It is well for us to remember that this is an opportunity to do something especially fine for our girls and the community at

large. The undertaking of a project of such magnitude does not occur everyday.

It is well to recall, too, that your prospects are the top fifteen per cent (15%) of the community.

6 How much will this trip cost you?

"It takes money to make money."
—American maxim

Many charities suffer from the advanced disease known as "penny-pincher's delight." This disease has many symptoms:

1. Operating with second-hand furnishings in a second-class office, with used equipment and personnel who are hired not for their abilities, but for their love of the organization.
2. Using as many volunteers as possible in any kind of work activity.
3. Avoiding spending the money on a new deferred giving program (or other type of potentially income-producing program) because it will produce income in the future, not today.
4. Avoiding any new kinds of programs or services on the grounds that we don't know enough about what kind of response we will get.
5. Avoiding the raising of any venture capital to explore new and different programs and services.
6. Crying loudly when the yearly budget is not met, including telling donors that if they don't give more this year, that we will go out of business!

7. Trying to raise money for endowment purposes, or even worse, trying to raise money "just to have a little surplus."

There are many other symptoms of this disease, but they all amount to the same thing: an unwillingness on the part of charities to confront the necessity of spending money in order to make money.

Let's take a very simple situation: a professional fund-raiser proposes three programs to your organization. You must choose which one you think would be best.

In Program A:

Cost:	$3,000	
Income:	$5,000	
Net:	+$2,000	(profit)

In Program B:

Cost:	$3,000	
Income:	$3,000	
Net:	-0-	(break-even)

In Program C:

Cost:	$3,000	
Income:	$1,500	
Net:	-$1,500	(loss)

Most of you would choose Program A as the only acceptable program. If that's what you would choose, run to the nearest doctor, for you exhibit the symptoms of the Charity Disease.

The correct answer is that there is not enough information. You are making a fundamental error when you assume that donors do not give money more than once. Or to put it another way, many organizations, thinking themselves conservative, agree not to finance any programs which are not self-sufficient in their first year. Such conservatism is misplaced and wrong. Often this kind of thinking does irreparable damage to an organization by making it tradition-bound and inflexible.

What you need in this example is another calculation step: How much will the donors give in future years?

When you consider the question of donor life (how long will a donor continue to give?), you enter the whole area of investment spending for non-profit organizations. If you know the length of your donor's life (or how much money you will receive from a donor over his giving life) you will then be able to decide how much you can afford to spend to get a new donor. An analysis of your present donors will give you the necessary information, and you will be able to make rational and logical choices.

This is the basic theory: Donors have a definite life. They give more than once. Further: There is no organization whose donors will not give more than once. And even: There is almost no way you can *prevent* donors from contributing more than once to your organization.

How is the donor life determined? This is really very simple, requiring only a statistical sampling of a group of donors. In other words, you can find out what the donor life of your organization is through experience, empirically. Through a sampling of a group of donors, you can *predict* how future donors will behave, and you will be able to make investment decisions accordingly.

There are three basic methods you can use to figure donor life.

1. *Exact method:* Select a group of donors (100 minimum) who started giving in the same year (say 1965) and record how many of that same group continued to give in each succeeding year. In other words, by actual examination of your records, find out how the same hundred donors behaved year after year. The farther back in time you go to select the initial sample, the farther you will be able to graph the results and the more reliable your results will be. Do this selection process for several different groups of donors in different years to make your results as statistically sound as possible. You should then graph the behavior of this sample group of a hundred donors. Compare your results with Graph A.

2. *Approximation method:* Instead of following the behavior of the same group of the same hundred donors (because of insufficient or inaccurate records), take a random sample of any year's donors (even last year's) and determine how many continued to give in the first year they were asked to contribute again. Take another sampling (you can use the same group or another group) of another year and see how many continued to give. Assume that the percentage that renewed that year remain constant.

3. *Assumption method:* Look at the chart below and decide which charity you are most like. Assume that your Donor Life Curve is the

same as those general types here. But be sure to start keeping adequate records so you can make your curve more accurate.

Type of Organization	*First Year-Donor Renewal Percentage*	*Each Succeeding Year-Donor Renewal Percentage*
1. Strong alumni organization, or prestige cultural or community organization	95%	95%
2. Average college or cultural organization	90%	90%
3. Strong fund-raiser with sophisticated philosophical appeal	75%	90%
4. Average fund-raiser with philosophical appeal	65%	85%
5. Fund-raiser with unsophisticated emotional appeal (sympathy causes)	50%	80%
6. Philosophical appeal fund-raiser with knowledge factors that tend to turn people "on" or "off"	50%	90%

Any of these three methods of figuring your Donor Life will give you a Donor Life Curve similar to the ones here.

Donor Life Curve Type A is one which results when 90 to 95 per cent of the initial group of a hundred donors renew their membership contributions in the first year they're asked. This curve also says that 90 to 95 per cent of the group remaining renew in each succeeding year. Basically, Type A charities have extremely loyal members.

It is theoretically possible to have a curve that is a straight line. In that case, the initial group of a hundred donors are so loyal they would renew every year until they died and may continue after death (through wills and bequests)! Needless to say, this kind of Donor Life isn't found very often. In many cases, it's only possible for a Donor Life Curve to go down (i.e., you will loose a certain amount of donors each year, if only because a certain number will move or die, or stop giving for personal reasons).

Donor Life Curve Type A is characteristic of four types of organizations:

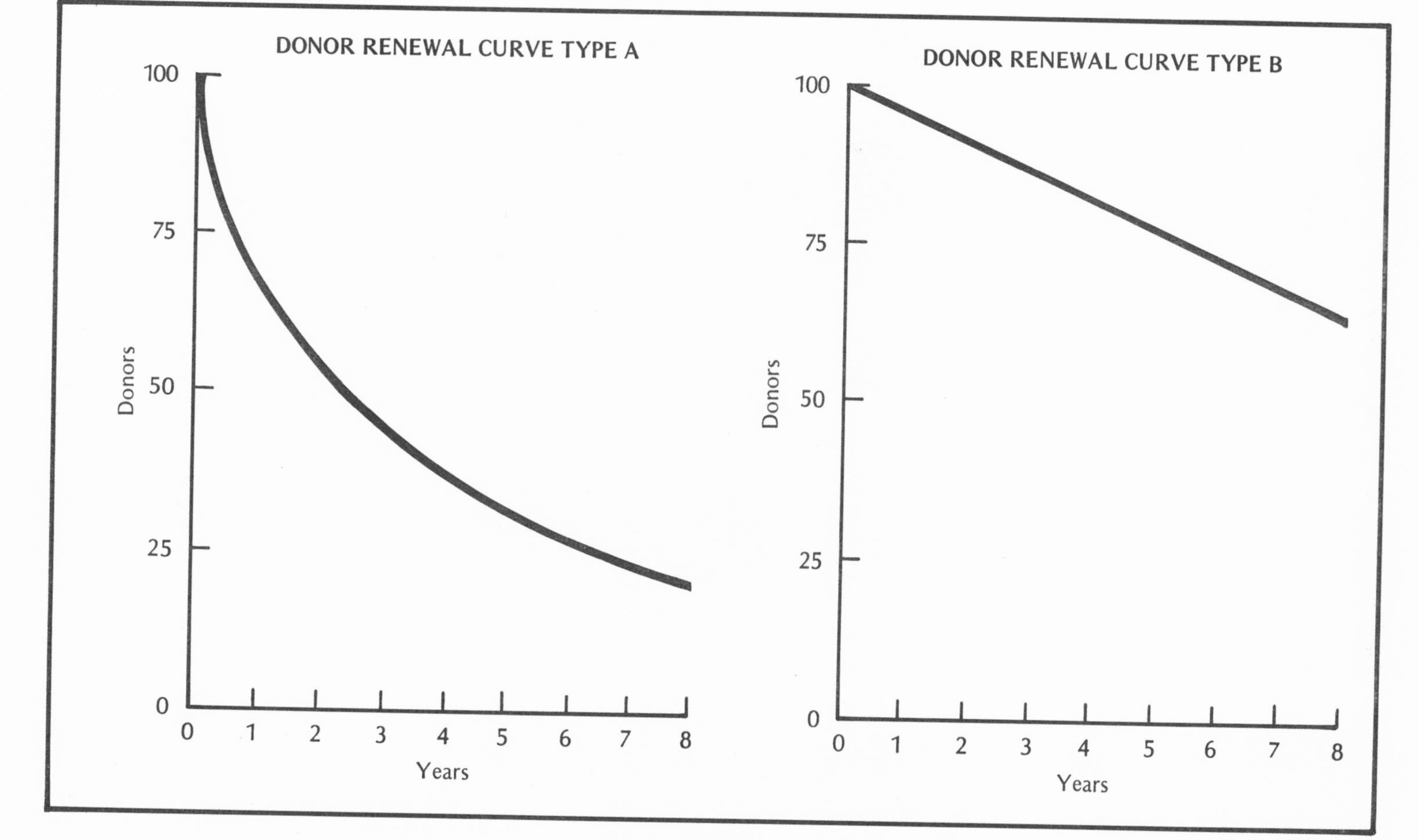
DONOR RENEWAL CURVE TYPE A
Donors
100
75
50
25
0
0 1 2 3 4 5 6 7 8
Years
DONOR RENEWAL CURVE TYPE B
Donors
100
75
50
25
0
0 1 2 3 4 5 6 7 8
Years

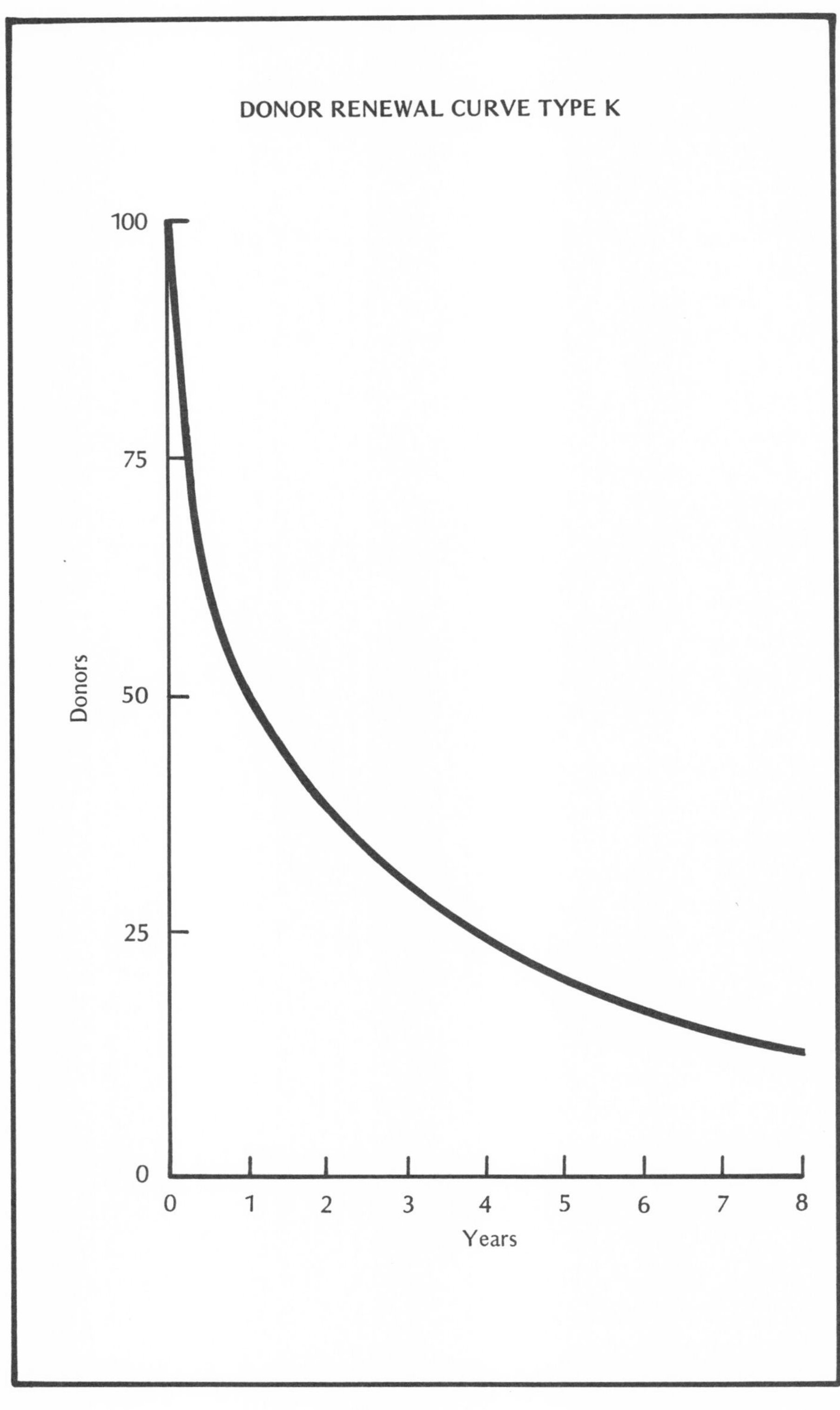
DONOR RENEWAL CURVE TYPE K
100
75
50
25
0
Donors
0
1
2
3
4
5
6
7
8
Years

1. Universities
2. Hospitals
3. Churches
4. Prestige cultural organizations

Type A charities have donors who will continue to give "religiously" over many, many years. A phenomenon that occurs in such organizations is the "death hump" which you can see in Donor Life Curve Type A. Donors to Type A organizations are so loyal that the donors must die before they will stop giving. In a very real sense, you can think of these Donor Life Curves as "Loyalty Curves," for loyalty is what they measure.

One of the consequences of having a "death hump" in your organization is that you should have a deferred giving program. If you have a "death hump" and don't have a deferred giving program, you aren't allowing your donors to express the full measure of their loyalty to you. And you are overlooking a potentially large source of revenue for your organization.

If you don't have a "death hump," this doesn't mean you shouldn't have a deferred giving program. Almost any organization can profit by including a deferred giving program in their overall fund-raising plan, but those with Donor Life Curve Type A will benefit especially from it.

Donor Life Curve Type B is typical of most charities. Here, 65 to 75 per cent of the initial donors renew their contributions in the first year, and 85 to 90 per cent of those remaining renew in each succeeding year. This curve is characterized by its "averageness." Donors are not extremely loyal, nor are they extremely unloyal. Most health, welfare, and youth organizations fall into this category.

Donor Life Curve Type K is called the "Kinky Cause Curve" because of the "kink" which occurs in the first year of renewal. Only 50 per cent renew their contributions in the first year, while 80 to 90 per cent renew each succeeding year. What causes the other 50 per cent to leave the folds of your charity in the first year? Normally, they leave because you feel you must flaunt your dirty linen in front of new donors. That is to say, you feel you must tell your new donors what you're doing and how you're spending their money. You typically pick (almost unerringly) the most controversial of your activities to publicize, instead of the most universal. You invite donors to disagree with the organizations' activities by explaining a lot that donors don't even want to know.

All of these Donor Life Curves come from the basic character of the organization itself, not the various fund-raising techniques you use. In other words, an organization with Type K Donor Life Curve could not, through using a better technique, change its curve to Type A. Slight variations are possible, but major variations are not.

Your organization should be similar to these general types. When you actually figure your "loyalty rate" you may find that it is somewhat irregular (i.e., 86 per cent the first year and 78 per cent each succeeding year, etc.), but that would not be unusual and should not disturb you.

Once you have determined your Donor Life Curve, you are ready to figure how many donations you will receive over future years. This is a simple mathematical calculation, as can be seen in the following example.

Donor Renewal Rate	Number of Original Donations	Number of Future Donations
95% / 95%	100	639.5
95% / 90%	100	512.4
75% / 90%	100	427.3
65% / 85%	100	315.2
50% / 80%	100	208.1
50% / 90%	100	284.8

Therefore, in Donor Life Curve Type B, every hundred donations received today will result in 315 future donations (over an eight-year period). If you make the same calculations for all of the general types of Donor Life Curves, you will arrive at the following table.

DONOR LIFE CURVE TYPE B

Year	1	2	3	4	5	6	7	8
First Year Donor Renewal Percentage	65%							
Each Succeeding Year Donor Renewal Percentage		85%	85%	85%	85%	85%	85%	85%
Number of Donations	65.0	55.3	47.0	39.9	33.9	28.8	24.5	20.8
Cumulative Total	65.0	120.3	167.3	207.2	241.1	269.9	294.4	315.2

The next step is to divide the *number* of future donations by the *number* of original donations to arrive at donor life. This is expressed by the formula:

$$FD \div OD = DL$$

If you do this on the table above, the result is:

Donor Renewal Rate	Donor Life
95% / 95%	6.4
90% / 90%	5.1
75% / 90%	4.3
65% / 85%	3.2
50% / 80%	2.0
50% / 90%	2.8

From this data, you can see that, in the case of Donor Life Curve Type B (65 per cent/85 per cent), for every donation we receive today, we will receive 3.2 future donations (over the life of the donor).

The next step is to calculate the average donation in the original year. This is expressed by the formula:

$$T\$ \div ND = AD$$

T$ stands for the total amount of dollars received; ND for the number of donations; AD for the average donation per donor. Let's pick a figure to work with: $10.00 average donation.

By multiplying the Donor Life (3.2 in our Type B example) times the average donation ($10.00) you get a total future income from each donor of $32.00. However, this is deceptive, because you are assuming donors will contribute the same amount, year after year. And this does not always happen.

In fact, what does happen is that donors, over their lives, give *more* money to the charities they support. Over a period of time, they *increase* their actual dollar amount of donations. There are many reasons for this, including these:

1. The donor makes more money (he gets raises in pay.)
2. The donor experiences a rise in economic status (he gets a promotion with a proportionate increase in salary).
3. Sometimes the donor becomes more involved with the charity (the charity's work becomes more important to him, so he contributes more money).
4. The donor has more "disposable income" (he has extra money that he does not urgently need to satisfy his living requirements).
5. Inflation.

Because of these factors, donors increase their gifts overtime and you must take this into account in your calculations. In the example, Donor Life Curve Type B, you can do this by looking at the average donation 3.2 years after the original year. Making the same calculation as before (T$ ÷ ND = AD), you find $13.00 to be our average donation in the year you have selected.

The next step is to divide the Average Future Donation (AFD) by the Average Original Donation (AOD) to arrive at the Increase Ratio (IR). This is expressed by the formula:

$$AFD \div AOD = IR$$

In the Type B example, this would be $13.00 ÷ $10.00 = 1.3. The Increase Ratio is 1.3.

But what if you perform this calculation and don't have an increase? This is a very real possibility. If you find that to be true, you must look to yourself to see what you're doing to frustrate donors' attempts to give you more money. They, as a group, have a natural upgrade rhythm, and this is frequently frustrated by your not asking them to give more money. Sometimes you do the same thing by asking for the same amount of money each year. If you have the same average donation year after year, or even a Decrease Ratio, you must take immediate steps to correct this situation.

There is only one remaining step to take before you can use this information data in an actual decision-making situation. That step is to express all of these figures in terms of constant dollars. Thus far, in the Type B example, you have:

Donor Life: 3.2
Average Original Donation: $10.00
Increase Ratio: 1.3

If you multiply all of them together you get $41.60, which is the total amount of dollars you will receive from each donor over his life. However, these future dollars will not have as much buying power, so you must adjust these future dollars accordingly. You can do this by using a discount rate of 5 per cent. Many economists believe that this is the annual rate at which the purchasing power of the dollar is diminishing. On page 156 is a discount table (at 5 per cent compounded annually).

Applying discount rate to your Type B example, you find that $41.60 (of future dollars) is worth $28.16 in terms of todays' dollars. For every donation of $10.00 you receive today, you will get $28.16 more (in constant dollars).

You can find the Total Income (TI) by using this two-step formula:

1. Donor Life × Average Donation × Increase Ratio × 5% Discount Rate = Future Income From Each Donor (in present terms)

In the Type B example:

3.2	×	$10.00	×	1.3	×	.677	=	$28.16

2. Future Income From Each Donor (in present terms) + Average Original Donation = Income From Each Donor (in present terms)

In the Type B example:

$28.16	+	$10.00	=	$38.16

Present Value of $1.00 Receivable at the End of Each Period

	Percentage									
Year	1	2	3	4	5	6	7	8	9	10
1	.990	.980	.971	.962	.952	.943	.935	.926	.917	.909
2	.980	.961	.943	.925	.907	.890	.873	.857	.842	.826
3	.971	.942	.915	.889	.864	.840	.816	.794	.772	.751
4	.961	.924	.888	.855	.823	.792	.763	.735	.708	.683
5	.951	.906	.863	.822	.784	.747	.713	.681	.650	.621
6	.942	.888	.837	.790	.746	.705	.666	.630	.596	.564
7	.933	.871	.813	.760	.711	.665	.623	.583	.547	.513
8	.923	.853	.789	.731	.677	.627	.582	.540	.502	.467
9	.914	.837	.766	.703	.645	.592	.544	.500	.460	.424
10	.905	.820	.744	.676	.614	.558	.508	.463	.422	.386
11	.896	.804	.722	.650	.585	.527	.475	.429	.388	.350
12	.887	.788	.701	.625	.557	.497	.444	.397	.356	.319
13	.879	.773	.681	.601	.530	.469	.415	.368	.326	.290
14	.870	.758	.661	.577	.505	.442	.388	.340	.299	.263
15	.861	.743	.642	.555	.481	.417	.362	.315	.275	.239
16	.853	.728	.623	.534	.458	.394	.339	.292	.252	.218
17	.844	.714	.605	.513	.436	.371	.317	.270	.231	.198
18	.836	.700	.587	.494	.416	.350	.296	.250	.212	.180
19	.828	.686	.570	.475	.396	.331	.277	.232	.194	.164
20	.820	.673	.554	.456	.377	.312	.258	.215	.178	.149
21	.811	.660	.538	.439	.359	.294	.242	.199	.164	.135
22	.803	.647	.522	.422	.342	.278	.226	.184	.150	.123
23	.795	.634	.507	.406	.326	.262	.211	.170	.138	.112
24	.788	.622	.492	.390	.310	.247	.197	.158	.126	.102
25	.780	.610	.478	.375	.295	.233	.184	.146	.116	.092
30	.742	.552	.412	.308	.231	.174	.131	.099	.075	.057

In order to figure our net income, however, it's necessary to subtract all applicable expenses, including the costs of soliciting future donations. For the purposes of this discussion, let's assume this figure is $1.00. It can be broken down as follows:

List maintenance	10¢
Renewal solicitations	30¢
Newsletters	30¢
Receipts	15¢
Staff overhead	15¢
Total	$1.00

These are hypothetical figures, of course, but they reflect the types of expenses which ought to be included in such computations. You can determine the actual figure for your organization by empirical examination of your expense records.

Now that you know (or can find out) how much a donor is worth to you over his life, you can now get to the important part. Knowing how much a donor is worth will allow you to decide how much you can spend in order to get a new donor. Or, to put it another way, knowing how much a donor is worth will tell you how much to spend on a prospect to get him to become a donor.

One area in which you can be helped by this information is that of postage. Most charities never stop to consider the possibility of using first class postage on a mailing to prospects because they want to save money. This urge for you to be frugal on behalf of your organization can have disastrous consequences, as you can see in the test below.

Test: Whether to use non-profit organization postage or first class postage on a mailing to prospects

In this test, the example has been weighted in favor of first class postage. You should *not* interpret this to mean that you should, from now on, use nothing but first class postage on all prospect mailings. What it does mean is you should test results in your own organization to see which works best for you. What you shouldn't do is *automatically* assume that non-profit organization postage should be used just because it's cheaper.

In a sense, the U.S. Postal Service has done a disservice to charities by creating the class of postage called non-profit, because most organizations, once granted this privilege, feel automatically compelled to use it. You should not use it everytime, and you should be sure to question which class of postage should be used in every different situation.

Even though it's tempting, and even though other direct mail experts try to give you the exact answer, it's not possible for anyone to tell you exactly which class of postage, or even which postage format (i.e., pre-printed indicia, metered, stamped, commemorative stamped, pre-cancelled 2 cent stamp, etc.) to use. The only way you can decide is to test these possible variations in your own specific situations. In other words, the only way for you to make any meaningful decision in this area is to test. Test, test, test!

Donor Life	3.2
Average original donation	$10.00
Increase ratio	1.3
Discount rate (compounded annually)	5%
Costs (of future solicitations)	$1.00

This is our original data from our Type B Donor Life Curve and other sources. Other data includes:

1. Costs of the mailings
2. Response rate

In the case of non-profit organization postage, the costs break down somewhat this way:

List rental (3¢ each) per 1,000 pieces	$ 30.00
Package (7¢ each) per 1,000 pieces	70.00
Postage (1.7¢ each) per 1,000 pieces	17.00
Total	$117.00

For first class postage, the mailing costs would be quite similar:

List rental (3¢ each) per 1,000 pieces	$ 30.00
Package (7¢ each) per 1,000 pieces	70.00
Postage (8¢ each) per 1,000 pieces	80.00
Total	$180.00

For comparison purposes, please note: There is a 54 per cent increase in cost when first class postage is used. The only variation in the two cases is the postage cost. However, this increase in postage cost is substantially higher than the increase in the response rate, as you see:

Non-profit response rate (1.5 per cent per 1000 pieces): 15

First class response rate (2.0 per cent per 1000 pieces): 20

Also, for comparison purposes, please note: This is a 33 per cent increase in response when first class postage is used.

This is where the example has been weighted. Basically, I am assuming that using first class postage will get a larger response. Why should this be so? First, approximately 20 per cent of the population of the United States moves annually. And it has been estimated that 60 to 80 per cent of those people move within the same county. Non-profit mail is not forwarded and first class mail is. Therefore, if more people receive the mail, more will open it, so more will respond.

The second reason I have assumed that first class mail will get a larger response is that it *is* first class mail, and people tend to open first class mail. Or to put it another way, people today tend to notice postage more than in the past. And this works two ways. Not only are they interested in seeing who would spend 8 cents to mail a letter to them, but also they are uninterested in finding out who is spending only 1.7 cents postage to reach them. So the second reason is that people tend to pay more attention to first class mail and less attention to non-profit mail. Perhaps the negative impact of non-profit mail is caused by the recipient's being able to predict what he'll find inside.

Even with these two valid reasons in support of first class mail, it's possible to offset them completely. The way you can do this is to put the words "Return Address Correction Requested" just under the organization's return address on the upper left-hand corner of the outside envelope. However, then you must make many other calculations which would complicate this example unnecessarily. Some of the calculations you would have to make here are:

1. 12 cents cost per piece of each address correction received by the organization.
2. 12 cents cost per piece for each list change (on the master file). This figure could be higher or lower depending on what your actual list changing costs are.
3. 7 cents cost per piece for a new package to send to the corrected addresses.
4. 10 cents postage per piece to send it out again. (U.S. postage regulations prohibit the use of 1.7 cents (non-profit postage) unless there are at least 200 pieces to go into the mail at the same time.)

This is a total of 41 cents of new cost per piece returned, and the percentage increase in response rate of the re-mailed packages would have to be very great to justify the extra costs involved. For simplicity, I have assumed that "Return Address Correction Requested" was not put on the outside envelope.

If we then multiply the Response Rate (number of donors) in each case times the Total Income from each donor in Donor Life Curve Type B, we find:

1. *Non-Profit Mail*:

Income From Each Donor	×	Number of Donors	=	Total Income From All Donors
$38.16	×	15	=	$572.40

2. *First Class Mail*:

Income From Each Donor	×	Number of Donors	=	Total Income From All Donors
$38.16	×	20	=	$763.20

From the total income, we must subtract the expenses:

1. *Non-Profit Mail*:

Original Mailing Cost	+	{ Donor Life	×	Costs (of future solicitations)	×	Response Rate }	=	Expens[e]
$117.00	+	{3.2	×	$1.00	×	15}	=	$165.0[0]

2. *First Class Mail*:

Original Mailing Cost	+	{ Donor Life	×	Costs (of future solicitations)	×	Response Rate }	=	Expens[e]
$200.00	+	{3.2	×	$1.00	×	20}	=	$264.0[0]

After figuring the expenses, you can now calculate the net income (after all expenses have been deducted).

1. *Non-Profit Mail*:

Total Income	−	Expenses	=	Net Income (profit)
$572.40	−	$165.00	=	$407.40

2. *First Class Mail*:

Total Income	−	Expenses	=	Net Income (profit)
$763.20	−	$264.00	=	$499.20

There is another calculation that must be made to bring these figures into full perspective, however. This entire example has been based so far on a simple mailing to 1000 prospects. To make this more realistic, we must multiply the results obtained by the total number of prospects available to the charity. In direct mail, the term for the total number of prospects available is "list universe." In this case, we will assume a list universe of 100,000 names.

1. *Non-Profit Mail*:

Net Income	×	List Universe	=	Total Life Income
$407.40	×	100,000	=	$407,400

2. *First Class Mail*:

Net Income	×	List Universe	=	Total Life Income
$499.20	×	100,000	=	$499,200

I'll be blunt. Under the mistaken impression of trying to save your organization some money (by using non-profit postage), you would have deprived it of $96,800 over the life of the donors. This is unforgivable. In this case, you could only make the correct decision if you had made all of the calculation steps. For you to have stopped at any point along the way would've resulted in a wrong decision.

Two further points must be discussed in this example. One is the concept of ethics in fund-raising and the other is the concept of risk. The ethical question is: What percentage of the funds raised for a charity should be spent on the costs of the solicitation program? In other words, what are the guidelines for acceptability of fund-raising costs? The risk question is: how much risk should a charity be allowed to take? The risk question is closely tied to the ethics question, and the same basic standards apply.

According to the *Harvard Business Review*, fund-raising costs in the first five years of an organization's existence, should average 25 per cent of the total amount of funds collected. After five years, this percentage should drop to 15 to 20 per cent. Professional fund-raisers often end capital funds and other types of campaigns with expenses falling between 12 to 15 per cent. Certainly 15 per cent is a good all-round rule of thumb.

Some fund-raising organizations, however, have costs which far exceed these standards. Some are 40 per cent and above. And some even run 85, 90, or 95 per cent! Frequently this type of organization receives a great deal of adverse publicity, and donations drop sharply. Organizations whose costs run in excess of 50 per cent of monies received ought to reexamine their fund-raising program to see if they could find another source of funds.

Hand in hand with this question of ethics is the problem of risk. It happens when fund-raising costs are too high. It's obvious that when fund-raising costs are quite high (say 75 per cent, for example) the risk of failure is also quite high. And conversely, when the fund-raising costs are low (say 15 per cent) the risk of failure is quite low. Non-profit organizations have a responsibility to see that most of the money a donor contributes actually goes for the cause. And, the non-profit organization needs to be cautious in its risk-taking activities. But being cautious in this case means keeping expenses at a minimum compared to the income received. It does not mean that you shouldn't take risks. You should only take well thought-out risks. In the preceding example, a well thought-out risk would be one which advocated the use of first class postage instead of non-profit postage.

In the cases above, both are acceptable from a risk and ethics point-of-view. In the final analysis, however, the first class postage must be utilized because of its superior income-producing potential.

A final word concerning the use of the Donor Life principle in other fund-raising situations: In the case cited above, you could do the mathematics easily and you could make a decision. It was easy because we used an example from direct mail, an area that you are accustomed to keeping statistical records. But what about other areas of fund-raising?

The Donor Life principle works well in any fund-raising situation in which accurate records are kept. This means you can apply it even in a major gift program, but you have to take time and effort to develop the necessary information. The principle of Donor Life will work in any situation where there are at least a hundred donors (or a large enough sample to be statistically reliable). Potential areas for use are: Major gift programs, deferred giving programs, corporate gift programs, membership drives, annual giving programs, to some extent foundation grant programs (if there is a large enough sample to work with), and, of course, a direct mail program.

The point: Investment decisions in non-profit organizations should never be made on the basis of just one year's return. Remember that donors have a life. They will give more than once. Any investment decision which does not take this factor into account is incomplete and misleading.

Bibliography

Bibliography

ACCOUNTING, DEFERRED GIVING AND TAXES

Accounting for Nonprofit Organizations, Emerson O. Henke, Wadsworth Publishing Co., $3.50.

Bequest Program Handbook, William E. Sheppard, Fund-Raising Institute, Plymouth Meeting, Pa., 1970, $10.00.

Commerce Clearing House, 351 California Street, San Francisco, California 94104 (publishes technical information on taxes and regulations relating to tax-exempt organizations).

The Complete Estate Planning Guide, Robert Brosterman, Mentor Book, 1970. New York, $1.50 (Chapter 17: "It Pays to Be Charitable").

Deferred Giving, American Alumni Council, Washington, D.C., $2.50 members, $3.50 non-members.

Estate Planning in Gift Development, Newkirk Associates, Inc., Professional Education Division, 308 Wolf Road, Latham, New York 12110, 1972, $96.00.

Fund Accounting, H. D. Kerrigan, McGraw-Hill, 1969, Text edition $12.95, Instructors' manual $3.50, Assignment manual $2.95.

Legal Aspects of Charitable Trusts and Foundations, Louis Lutner, Commerce Clearing House, 1970, $17.50.

Non-Profit Organizations, Financial and Accounting Guide, Malvern J. Gross, Jr. Ronald, 1972, $13.50.

Philanthropy Tax Institute, 280 Park Avenue, New York, New York 10017 (Free information on tax aspects of giving).

The Tax Climate for Philanthropy, T. Willard Hunter, American College Public Relations Association, 1 Dupont Circle, Washington, D.C. 20036, 1968, $5.75 ($2.75 in paperback).

Tax Impacts on Philanthropy, Tax Institute of America (Symposium), Tax Institute of America, 457 Nassau Street, Princeton, N.J. 08540, 1972, $15.00.

Taxes and Estates, Wells Fargo Bank, Trust Department, 464 California Street, San Francisco, California 94104. (monthly newsletter, free.)

Taxes for Fund-Raisers, Business Reports Inc., 1 West Avenue, Larchmont, New York (newsletter), monthly, $36.00 yearly.

Taxwise Giving Newsletter, Taxwise Giving, 280 Park Avenue, New York, New York 10017, published monthly, $45.00 per year.

ADVERTISING

Advertising, John S. Wright and Daniel S. Warner, McGraw-Hill, New York, 1962, $8.50.

Advertising—A New Approach, Walter Taplan, Little, Brown, 1960, $5.00.

Advertising Copywriting, Phillip W. Burton and G. Bowman Kreer, Prentice-Hall (2nd Edition), Englewood Cliffs, New Jersey, 1961, $7.95.

Advertising Handbook, Roger Barton, Prentice-Hall, Englewood Cliffs, New Jersey.

Advertising Principles and Problems, Charles J. Kirksen and Arthur Kroegger, Richard D. Irwin Co., Homewood, Illinois, 1960, $10.65.

Advertising Procedure, Otto Kleppner, Prentice-Hall (5th Edition), Englewood Cliffs, New Jersey, 1966.

Advertising Psychology and Research, Darrell B. Lucas & Stewart H. Britt, McGraw-Hill, New York, 1950, $8.95.

Advertising Techniques and Management, Robert V. Zacher, Richard D. Irwin, Inc., Homewood, Illinois, 1961, $10.65.

Advertising to Business, Roland B. Smith, Richard D. Irwin, Inc., Homewood, Ill., 1957, $10.00.

Confessions of an Advertising Man, David Ogilvy, Ballantine Books, New York, N.Y., 1963, $1.25.

The Copywriters' Guide, Elbrun R. French, Harper & Row, New York, 1959, $11.95.

Effects of Mass Communication, Joseph T. Klapper. The Free Press, 866 Third Avenue, New York, N.Y. 10022, 1960, $5.95.

Exploring Advertising, Otto Kleppner & Irving Settel, Prentice-Hall, Englewood Cliffs, N.J., 1970, $5.95.

Handbook of Advertising Art Production, Richard A. Schlemmer, Prentice-Hall, Inc., 1966.

How Advertising is Written—and Why, Aesop Glim. Dover Publications, Inc., New York, 1954, $2.00.

How to Manage Industrial Advertising, Franklin W. Bartle, Printers' Ink Pub. Co., New London, Conn., 1955, $3.95.

How to Write a Good Advertisement, Victor O. Schwab, Harper & Row, New York, 1962, $5.95.

How to Write Advertising That Sells, Clyde O. Bedell, McGraw-Hill Book Co., New York, 1952, $12.50, (second edition).

Industrial Advertising, Frederick R. Messner, McGraw-Hill, New York, 1963, $8.75.

Merchandising for Tomorrow, Edward B. Weiss, McGraw-Hill, New York, 1961, $7.50.

Motivation in Advertising, Pierre Martineau, McGraw-Hill Paperbacks, New York, 1957, $2.95.

My First Sixty Years in Advertising, Maxwell Sackheim. Prentice-Hall, Inc., Englewood Cliffs, N.J., 1970, $20.00.

On the Writing of Advertising, Walter Weir, McGraw-Hill, New York, 1960, $6.75.

Retail Advertising and Sales Promotion, Charles M. Edwards, Jr. & Russell A. Brown, Prentice-Hall, New York, 1959. $8.75.

Tested Advertising Copy, Carroll J. Swan, Printers' Ink, New London, Conn., 1955, $6.00.

Tested Advertising Methods, John Caples, Harper & Row, New York, 1961, (revised edition) $6.95.

THE ARTS

The Arts in Boston, Bernard Taper. Harvard University Press, Cambridge, Mass. 02138, 1970, $6.00 ($2.95 in paperback).

Grants and Aid to Individuals in the Arts, Washington International Arts Letter, 115 Fifth St., S.E., Washington, D.C. 20003, 1970, $8.95.

Private Foundations Active in the Arts, Washington International Arts Letter. 115 Fifth Street, S.E., Washington, D.C. 20003, 1970, $17.50.

The State of the Arts and Corporate Support, Gideon Chagy (ed.), Paul S. Erickson, Inc., 1971, $10.00.

CORPORATIONS

Company Giving, Leo Shapiro, Ph.D. Survey Press, 814 North Michigan Ave., Chicago, Ill. 60611, 1960, $5.75.

Corporate Support Programs to Institutions of Higher Learning, Jack J. Holder, Jr., Interstate, 1967, $2.50.

The Corporation and the Arts, Richard Eells. Macmillan Company, 866 Third Avenue, New York, N.Y. 10022, 1967, $7.95.

The Manual of Corporate Giving, Bearsley Ruml, ed. National Planning Association, 1606 New Hampshire Avenue, N.W., Washington, D.C. 20009, 1952, $6.75.

1970 Corporation Support of Higher Education Biennial Council for Financial Aid to Education, Inc., 6 East 45th Street, New York, N.Y. 10017, 1970, $2.00.

Policies Underlying Corporate Giving, Ralph L. Thomas, Prentice-Hall, Englewood Cliffs, N.J., 1965, $19.95.

Study of Company-Sponsored Foundations, Frank M. Andrews. Russell Sage Foundation, 230 Park Avenue, New York, N.Y. 10017, 1960, $1.50.

Twenty Company-Sponsored Foundations, National Industrial Conference Board, Inc., 845 Third Avenue, New York 10022, 1970, $17.50.

DIRECT MAIL

Building and Maintaining Industrial Direct Mail Lists, Marketing Communications Research Center, 1961, (Report #10).

Computer Handbook for Fund Raisers, 2nd Edition, Fund-Raising Institute. Box 122, Plymouth Meeting, Pa. 19462, 1970, $12.50.

Direct Mail and Direct Response Promotion, Christian Brann, Halsted-/Wiley, 1971, $13.75.

Direct Mail and Mail Order Handbook, Richard S. Hodgson, The Dartnell Corp., Chicago, Ill., 1965 (third printing, revised), $24.95.

Direct Mail Design International, R. A. Ballinger, Reinhold Pub. Co., New York, 1963, $15.00.

Direct Mail File of 100 Ideas, American Printer & Lithographer, Harry B. Coffin, Direct Mail Advertising Assoc., New York, $5.00.

Direct Mail Showmanship, Richard Hodgson, American Marketing Services, Waltham, Ma., 1961, $17.50.

Direct Marketing, (magazine) monthly, 224 Seventh St., Garden City, N.Y. 11530, $10.00.

Handbook of Industrial Direct Mail Advertising, Edward N. Mayer, Jr., and Roy G. Ljungren, Association of Industrial Advertisers, 41 E. 42nd St., New York, N.Y. 10017, 1972, $10.00.

Help Yourself to Better Mail Order, Robert A. Baker, Printers' Ink Pub. Company, New London, Conn., 1953, $6.50.

Henry Hoke Library, Reporter of Direct Mail Advertising, Garden City, N.Y., 10 volumes, $12.50.

1. Dogs That Climb Trees
2. How to Get the Right Start in Direct Advertising
3. How to Think About Direct Mail
4. How to Think About Letters
5. How to Think About Readership in Direct Mail
6. How Direct Mail Solves Management Problems
7. How to Think About Showmanship in Direct Mail
8. How to Think About Mail Order
9. How to Think About Production and Mailing
10. How to Think About Industrial Direct Mail

"How to Create Good Direct Mail in 10 Easy Steps", Mort Weiner, Reporter of Direct Mail Advertising, Garden City, New York, N.Y., May, 1960.

How to Get More for Your Direct Mail Dollar, Dickie-Raymond, Inc., 1957.

How to Make More Money with Your Direct Mail, Edward N. Mayer, Jr., Marketing Communications, Inc., New York, 1961, (fourth edition).

How to Start and Operate a Mail Order Business, Julian Simon, McGraw-Hill. New York, 1965, $8.95.

How to Start and Run a Successful Mail Order Business, Sean Martyn. David McKay Company, Inc., New York, 1969, $6.95.

Hub Mail, 1000 Washington St., Boston, Mass. 02118, (Publishes a fund-raising newsletter. Free on request.)

The KRC Manual of Computer Applications in Fund-Raising, KRC associates, 105 Mamaroneck Avenue, Mamaroneck, New York 10543, 1972, $30.00.

Measuring the Effectiveness of Industrial Direct Mail, Marketing Communications Research Center (all included in Report #14):

Study #1: Basic Factors Which Control Mailing Lists 1961

Study #2: Planning More Productive Mailings 1964

Study #3: Pretesting Industrial Direct Mail 1965

Membership Promotion Manual for Trade and Professional Associations, Alfred B. LaGasse & Walter L. Cook, American Society of Assn. Executives, 1972, $12.00, (revised edition).

"101 Tips for Direct Mail Advertising," Franklin C. Wertheim, *Advertising Requirements* (now *Promotion*), February, 1955. A Primer for Editors, American Alumni Council, Washington, D.C., $2.50.

Printing and Promotion Handbook, Daniel Melcher and Nancy Larrick, McGraw-Hill Book Co., New York, 1966, (third edition).

Successful Direct Mail Advertising and Selling, Robert Stone, Prentice-Hall, Englewood Cliffs, N.J., 1955, $5.75.

Testing—The Scientific Approach to Direct Mail, Dr. William Arkwright Doppler, Direct Mail Advertising Assoc., New York, N.Y., 1960, $5.00.

EDUCATIONAL FUND-RAISING

"Academic Fund Raising: Yesterday and Today." Courtney C. Brown, *School and Society* 93:240-2 (April 17, 1965).

Academic Process, Henry M. Wriston. Columbia University Press, 136 South Broadway, Irvington-on-Hudson, N.Y. 10533, 1959, $5.00.

"Academic Philanthropy: The Art of Getting," Gene R. Hawes, *Saturday Review*, 50:65-7 (December 16, 1967).

Aid-to-Education Programs of Some Leading Business Concerns. CFAE, 6 East 45th Street, New York, N.Y. 10017, 1970, $6.00.

Alma Mater, Journal of the American Alumni Council, Washington, D.C., $8.00, (periodical).

Alumni Administration: 50-College Study, American Alumni Council Washington, D.C., $2.50 members, $4.00 non-members.

Alumni Administration Awards Case Summaries, American Alumni Council, Washington, D.C., 1971, $2.50.

American Philanthropy for Higher Education: Gifts and Bequests to Fifty Selected Colleges and Universities, John Price Jones Company, New York (free).

Bulletin on Public Relations and Development for Colleges and Universities, Gonser, Gerber, Tinker Stuhr, Chicago, January, 1969.

Case Histories of Educational Fund-Raising, American Alumni Council, Washington, D.C., $1.00.

The Case for the Matching Gift: Matching Gift Details, American Alumni Council, Washington, D.C., $2.00.

Class Insurance Programs, American Alumni Council, Washington, D.C., $1.00.

College Development Bulletin, Gonser, Gerber, Tinker, Stuhr, 105 West Madison Street, Chicago, Ill. 60602, bi-monthly bulletin, free of charge.

"Developing Financial Resources," D. A. Eldridge, *Junior College Journal*, 35:28-31 (October, 1964).

Education and the Business Dollar, Kenneth G. Patrick and Richard Eells. The Macmillan Company, 866 Third Avenue, New York, N.Y. 10022, 1969, $8.95.

Financial Aid for Higher Education, Office of Education, U.S. Department of Health, Education, and Welfare, U.S. Government Printing Office, Washington, D.C. 20025, 1968, $1.00.

Financial Planning Model for Private Colleges, William J. Arthur, University Press of Virginia.

Focus on Understanding & Support: A Study in College Management, John W. Leslie. American College Public Relations Association, 1 Dupont Circle, Washington, D.C. 20036, 1969, $3.95.

The Fundamentals of Educational Fund-Raising, American Alumni Council, Washington, D.C., $1.50.

Fund-Raising for Higher Education, John A. Pollard, Harper & Bros., New York, $4.00.

The Handbook of Aid to Higher Education by Corporations, Major

Foundations, and the Federal Government, Council for Financial Aid to Education, 6 East 45th St., New York, N.Y. 10017, $25.00.

Handbook of College and University Administration, Asa S. Knowles, McGraw-Hall, New York, 1970.

"Increased Funds Are Available If . . ." Paul H. Davis, *Liberal Education*, (October, 1969), Vol. 55, p. 410.

Institutions in Transition/A Profile of Change in Higher Education, Carnegie Commission on Higher Education. McGraw-Hill Book Company, New York, 1971, $6.95.

Letter to a College President, Sidney G. Tickton. Ford Foundation, 320 East 43rd Street, New York 10017, 1963, free of charge.

Major Gift Societies, American Alumni Council, Washington, D.C., $1.50 members, $2.00 non-members.

Matching Gift Details, American Alumni Council, Washington, D.C., $2.00.

Needed: A Ten Year College Budget, Sidney G. Tickton. Fund for the Advancement of Education, 477 Madison Avenue, New York, N.Y. 10022, 1961, free of charge.

Papers in Educational Fund-Raising, American Alumni Council, Washington, D.C., $2.50 members, $3.50 non-members.

Patterns of Giving to Higher Education: An Analysis of Contributions and Their Relation to Tax Policy, Julian H. Levi and Fred S. Vorsanger, American Council on Education, 1 Dupont Circle, Washington, D.C. 20036, $2.00.

Philanthropy in Shaping American Education, Merle Curti. Rutgers University Press, 30 College Avenue, New Brunswick, N.J. 08903, 1963, $8.50.

Preliminaries to a Development Program, American Alumni Council, Washington, D.C., $1.00.

Private Universities in the Seventies, Committee for Corporate Support of American Universities. Room 1030, 825 Third Avenue, New York, N.Y. 10022, 1970, free of charge.

Some Aspects of Educational Fund Raising, Jean D. Linehan (ed.), American Alumni Council, Washington, D.C., 1961.

A Study of Voluntary Support For Public Community Colleges in New York State, Charles R. MacRoy, unpublished doctoral dissertation. State University of New York at Buffalo. February, 1970.

Survey of Voluntary Support of Education, American Alumni Council, Washington, D.C., $5.00.

Things I Wish They'd Told Me, American Alumni Council, Washington, D.C., $1.00.

The Vanishing Alumnus, American Alumni Council, Washington, D.C. $1.00.

Voluntary Support of Education, Council for Financial Aid to Education, Inc. CFAE, 6 East 45th Street, New York, N.Y. 10017, 1970-71, $5.00.

FOUNDATIONS

Annual Register of Grant Support, Academic Media, 32 Lincoln Avenue, Orange, New Jersey 07050, 1971, $39.50.

"Applications for Grants," F. Emerson Andrews. *Philanthropic Foundations* New York: Russell Sage Foundation, 1956, $10.00.

The Big Foundations, Waldemar A. Nielsen. Columbia University Press, 136 South Broadway, Irving-on-Hudson, N.Y. 10533, 1972, $10.95.

The Bread Game—The Realities of Foundation Fund-Raising. Glide Publications, 1973, $1.95.

A Comprehensive Guide to Successful Grantship, William J. Hill. Littleton, Colorado: Grant Development Institute, 1972. Looseleaf. $24.00.

Conference Proceedings, Council on Foundations, 393 Seventh Avenue, New York, New York 10001, annual, a service for foundations administering charitable funds for public purposes.

Conference on Foundations, November, 1970. Transcript free. Charles F. Kettering Foundation, 5335 Far Hills Avenue, Dayton, Ohio 45429.

Directory of European Foundations, Giovanni Agnelli Foundation, Russell Sage, 1969, $9.00.

Foundation Directory, published for the Foundation Center, 444 Madison Avenue, New York, New York 10022, by Columbia University Press, New York City; published irregularly latest in 1971, $18.00.

The Foundation Grants Index, 1970-71, Columbia University Press, 136 S. Broadway, Irving-on-Hudson, N.Y. 10533, $10.00.

Foundation News, published for the Foundation Center, bi-monthly, $6.00/year. Write Subscription Department, 428 East Preston Street, Baltimore, Maryland 21202.

Foundations Portfolio, Fund Raising Institute, Plymouth Meeting, Pa., 1970, $7.50.

Foundations, Private Giving and Public Policy: Report and Recommendations of the Commission of Foundations and Private Philanthropy, Peter G. Peterson and others. The University of Chicago Press, 1971, $12.50.

Foundations: Twenty Viewpoints, F. Emerson Andrews, Russell Sage Foundation, 230 Park Ave., New York, N.Y. 10017, $1.25.

Future Opportunities for Foundation Support, Olaf Helmer and Helen Helmer. Institute for the Future, Menlo Park, California, 1970.

How to Get Your Fair Share of Foundation Grants, Joseph Dermer (ed). Public Service Materials Center, 104 East 40th Street, New York, N.Y. 10016, 1973, $12.00.

How to Obtain Foundation Grants, Fred D. Knittle. R. L. Houts Associates, Inc., Los Angeles, 1972, $75.00.

How to Raise Funds from Foundations, Joseph Dermer, Public Service Materials Center, 104 East 40th Street, New York, New York 10016.

How to Write a Proposal, Michael MacIntyre, Education, Training, and Research Sciences Corp., Washington, D.C., 1971. 5500. $3.95.

How to Write Successful Foundation Presentations, Joseph Dermer, Public Service Materials Center, 104 East 40th Street, New York, New York 10016, $8.50.

Information Quarterly, the Foundation Center, Columbia University Press, Irving-on-Hudson, New York, N.Y. $7.50 year, (updated information on more than 2,000 foundations listed in *Foundation Quarterly*.)

Legal Instruments of Foundations, F. Emerson Andrews. Russell Sage Foundation, 230 Park Avenue, New York, N.Y. 10017, 1958, $6.50.

A Manual for Obtaining Foundation Grants, Louis A. Urgo, Robert J. Corcoran Co., Boston, Mass. 1971, $5.75.

The Money Givers, Joseph C. Goulden, Random House, 1971, $8.95. (all about foundations)

1970-71 Survey of Grant-Making Foundation with Assets of over $500,000, Public Service Materials Center, 104 E. 40th St., New York, N.Y. 10016, $7.50.

The 1972-73 Survey of Grant-Making Foundations with Assets of Over $500,000 or Grants of Over $25,000, Public Service Materials Center

Public Service Materials Center, 104 East 40th Street, New York, N.Y. 10016, 1972, $7.95.

Philanthropic Foundations in Latin America, Ann Strombert, Russell Sage Foundation, New York, 1968, $8.95.

Philanthropic Foundations, F. Emerson Andrews, Basic Books, 1956, $7.50.

Proceeding of the Sixth Biennial Conference on Charitable Foundations, New York University, Matthew Bender & Co., Marketing Dept., 235 E. 45th St., New York, N.Y. 10017, $10.50.

Seeking Foundation Funds, David Church, National Public Relations Council of Health and Welfare Services, 419 Park Avenue South, New York, New York 10016, $2.50.

Taft Information System, Taft Products, Inc., 1000 Vermont Avenue, N.W., Washington, D.C. 20005, $250.00 yearly.

Tax-Exempt Foundations: Their Impact on Small Business (Volume II: Appendix), U.S. Government Printing Office, Washington, D.C. 20402, 1972 (list of all foundations in U.S.), $9.00.

Understanding Foundations: Dimensions in Fund Raising, J. Richard Taft, McGraw-Hill, New York, 1967, $2.95.

U.S. Philanthropic Foundations: Their History, Structure, Management and Records, Warren Weaver, Harper & Row, New York, $7.95.

What You Must Know to Manage a Charitable Foundation Under the Tax Reform Act, Stanley Pressment. Panel Publishers, Inc., 14 Plaza Road, Greenvale, N.Y. 11548, 1970, $60.00 (includes supplements).

Where America's Large Foundations Make Their Grants, Joseph Dermer, Public Service Materials Center, 104 East 40th Street, New York, New York 10016, 1971, $19.50.

FUND-RAISING

Annual Giving Idea Book, William E. Sheppard, Fund-Raising Institute. Plymouth Meeting, Pa., 1972, $25.00.

"The Art of Fund-Raising," Harold N. Weiner, *Wilson Library Bulletin,* 42: 289-92 (November, 1967).

Casebook of Institutional Advancement Programs, American College Public Relations Assn., 1 Dupont Circle, Washington, D.C. 20036, $12.50.

Complete Fund-Earning Guide, J. Harris Pritchard. A.J.L. Publishing Company, Inc., 757 Third Avenue, New York, N.Y. 10017, 1967, $10.00.

The Complete Fund-Raising Guide, Howard R. Mirkin. Public Service Materials Center, 104 E. 40th St., New York, N.Y. 10016, $12.50.

Designs for Fund-Raising: Principles, Patterns, Techniques, Harold J. Seymour, McGraw-Hill, 1966, $6.95.

Final Report on the Princeton Capital Campaign, Princeton University Press, Princeton, N.J., 1959-62, free.

Fund-Raising (brochure), Student Mobilization Committee, 1029 Vermont Ave., N.W., Washington, D.C. 20005, $2.00 for 100.

Fund-Raising for Small Charities and Organizations, H. R. Humphries, David & Charles, 1972, $5.50.

Fund-Raising for the Small Organization, Phillip G. Sheridan, M. Evans, 1968, $5.95.

Fund-Raising Institute, Box 122, Plymouth Meeting, Pennsylvania 19462, (newsletter, bulletin, and letter clinic, $26.00/year).

Fund-Raising Made Easy, E. S. Newman and L. J. Margolin, Oceana, $1.50.

Fund-Raising Management, 224 Seventh Street, Garden City, New York 11530, $8.00/year/6 times per year, magazine.

Guides to Capital Financing of Hospitals, American Hospital Assn., 1962, $1.75.

Guide for Development, Hiram Phillips, Praeger, 1969, $15.00.

Guides to Successful Fund-Raising, Able A. Hanson, Teachers College, New York, 1961, $1.75.

Guide to Successful Fund-Raising Dinners, Edwin & Selma Field, 25 Landfield Ave., Monticello, N.Y. 12701, $14.95.

Handbook of Stewardship Procedures, Thompson, Prentice-Hall, Inc., Englewood Cliffs, N.J.

Handbook of Successful Fund-Raising, Paul C. Carter, Hawthorn, 1970, $19.95.

Help for the Small Museum, Armita Neal, Pruett, 1969, (second edition), $7.50.

"How Churches and Colleges Can Use the Tax Reform Act of 1969 to Make Fund Raising Easier," Report Bulletin #8, *Tax Exempt Organizations,* Prentice-Hall, Inc.

How Groups Raise Funds, Helen K. Knowles, The Bond Wheelwright Company, Freeport, Me., 1961.

"How to Ask Your Friends for Money," *Changing Times*, 21:35-7, (April, 1967).

How to Build a Long-Term Fund Program, Donald C. Carner. Motivation, Inc., P.O. Box 4695, Stamford, Conn. 06907, 1966, $5.95.

How to Raise Money for Community Action, Scholarship, Education and Defense Fund for Racial Equality, 164 Madison Ave., New York, N.Y. 10016, 25¢.

The KRC Handbook of Fund-Raising Strategy and Tactics, KRC Associates, 105 Mamaroneck Avenue, Mamaroneck, New York 10543, 1972, $30.00.

The KRC Letter, KRC Associates, 105 Mamaroneck Avenue, Mamaroneck, New York 10543, (newsletter), monthly, $30.00 yearly.

McCall's Book of Fund-Raising Ideas, Prentice-Hall, Marjorie Fatt Chester and Richard Marek, 1963.

"Money & How to Get It," *Behavior Today*. Del Mar, California (reprints of articles that appeared in 1971), $5.00.

Money-Raising Activities for Community Groups, Virginia W. Musselman, Association Press, 1969, $7.95.

National Society of Fund-Raisers Newsletter, 130 East 40th Street, New York, New York 10017, monthly, free.

One Hundred and One Ways to Raise Money for Your Church, Ralph Seaman, Fell Publishing Company, 1952, $2.00.

Philanthropic Fund Raising As a Profession, David M. Church. Bellman Publishing Company, P.O. Box 172, Cambridge, Mass. 02138, 1967, $1.25.

Proceedings of the Institute for Financial Development, Paul K. Preus, Memphis State University, 1972, $45.00.

Raising Money for Church Building Projects, Arthur W. Lumly. Abingdon Press, East 55th Street, New York, N.Y. 10022, 1954, $1.00.

So You're Going to Raise Funds, David M. Church. National Public Relations Council for Health & Welfare Services, 419 Park Avenue S, New York, N.Y. 10016, 1965, $1.25.

Some Methods of Telephone Solicitation, American Alumni Council, Washington, D.C., $1.00.

Techniques of Successful Fund Raising, Adam Gordon and Abbie Gordon, Exposition, 1967, $5.00.

Tested Methods in Fund-Raising, Publitex International Corporation, 509 General Know Road, King of Prussia, Pennsylvania 19406, 1968, $29.95.

Tested Methods of Raising Money: for Churches, Colleges and Health and Welfare Agencies, Margaret M. Fellows & Stella A. Koenig, Harper & Row, New York, N.Y., 1959, $6.95.

Ways and Means Handbook, The Sperry & Hutchinson Co., Consumer Services, P.O. Box 112, Fort Worth, Texas 76110, single copies free.

GENERAL

Giving, U.S.A., Bulletin, American Association of Fund-Raising Council, Inc., 500 Fifth Avenue, New York, New York 10036, yearly $12.50.

How to Become a Non-Profit Tax-Exempt Corporation, and Why, and Why Not, Law Commune, 347 Alma Street, Palo Alto, California 94301, Free.

Insights, Interpreting Institutions, P.O. Box 6897, Baltimore, Md. 21204 (periodical).

"Management of Nonprofit Organizations Series, *Harvard Business Review*. Cambridge, Mass.: Reprint No. 21123, $5.00.

National Information Bureau Inc., 305 East 45th Street, New York, New York 10017 (free index of services).

Nonprofit Report, 205 Main St., Danbury, Ct. 06810, monthly newsletter ($72.00 per year for non-profit organizations).

Nonprofit Research Group, P.O. Box 466, Ben Franklin Sta., Washington, D.C. 20044.

Philanthropic Digest, Brakeley, John Price Jones, Inc., 30 East 42nd Street, New York, New York 10017, (newsletter), 16 times a year, $10.00.

Organizations and Clients: Essays in the Sociology of Service, William R. Rosengren and Mark Lefton, Charles E. Merrill, Columbus, Ohio, 1970, $3.75.

The Organizer's Manual, The O.M. Collective, Bantam Books, New York, 1971, $1.25 (has a chapter on fund-raising).

The Professional Radical, Marion K. Sanders. Perennial Library, New York, 1965, $.95.

The Recruitment and Training of Development Directors (A Panel Dis-

cussion), Marts & Lundy, Inc., 521 Fifth Avenue, New York, N.Y. 10017, free of charge (limited supply available).

Reveille for Radicals, Saul D. Alinsky. Vintage Books, N.Y., 1946, $1.65.

Rules for Radicals, Saul D. Alinsky, Random House, 1971, $6.95 (community organizing).

Yearbook of American Churches, National Council of Churches of Christ in America, 475 Riverside Drive, New York, N.Y. 10027, $7.50.

Your Community Hospital, Robert E. Walsh. Beacon Press, 25 Beacon Street, Boston, Mass. 02108, 1969, $5.95.

GOVERNMENT GRANTS

Catalogue of Federal Domestic Assistance, Executive Office of the President, Government Printing Office, Washington, D.C. 20402, $7.25.

A Comprehensive Summary of Federal Loans, Grants and Contracts in Health, Education and Welfare Programs, Tamblyn & Brown, Inc. and T & B Public Grants Services, Inc. T & B, Inc., 1700 Pennsylvania Avenue, N.W., Washington, D.C. 20006, 1969, $1.00.

Grants-in-Aid to Voluntary Agencies: A Study of Procedures, Processes and Problems, Central Institute of Research and Training in Public Cooperation, International Publications Service, 1969, $4.00.

Grants Management: The Office of Education and State Education Agency, Burton D. Friedman, Pub. Admin, 1971, $3.00.

How to Apply for Grants, Marvin Rich, Scholarship, Education and Defense Fund for Racial Equality, 164 Madison Ave., New York, N.Y. 10016, 25¢.

Legally Available U.S. Government Information, Mathew J. Kerbec, Van Nostrand Reinhold, 1971, $86.00.

A Manual for Obtaining Government Grants, Louis A. Urgo, Robert J. Corcoran Co., Boston, Mass., $6.50, (third edition).

Millions for Arts: Federal and State Cultural Programs, Washington International Arts Letter, Washington, D.C., $10.50.

"Multiplying Services Through Government Grants and Contracts," United Way of America, Voluntarism Development Division, 801 N. Fairfax St., Alexandria, Va. 22313, Volume 2, January, 1972, $1.00.

Sharing Federal Funds for State and Local Needs: Grants-in-Aid and

PPB Systems. (Special Studies in U.S. Economic and Social Development), Selma J. Mushkin and Joseph F. Cotton, Praeger, N.Y., 1969, $11.00.

LETTER-WRITING

The Art of Clear Thinking, Rudolf Flesch, Collier Books/Macmillan Co., New York, 1951, $1.25.

The Art of Plain Talk, Rudolf Flesch, Collier Books/Macmillan Co., New York, 1951, 95¢.

The Art of Readable Writing, Rudolph Flesch, Collier Books/Macmillan Co., New York, 1949, $1.25.

The Business-Letter Deskbook, Gerald W. Weston, Dartnell Pub. Co., Chicago, Ill., 1963, $7.50, (revised edition).

Communications Through Letters and Reports, Jack H. Menning & C. W. Wilkinson, Richard D. Irwin, Inc., Homewood, Ill., 1963 (third edition), $7.95.

Correspondence Manual, Leslie Llewellyn Lewis & Marilyn French, Dartnell Publishing Co., Chicago, Ill., 1958, $7.50.

Effective Letters In Business, Robert L. Shurter, McGraw-Hill, New York, 1954, $5.95, (second edition).

The Fund-Raising Letter Collection, Fund Raising Institute, Plymouth Meeting, Pa. 19462, $25.00.

Handbook of Business Letters, L. E. Frailey, Prentice-Hall, Englewood Cliffs, N.J., $12.50.

How to Increase Sales with Letters, Earle A. Buckley, McGraw-Hill, New York, 1961, $5.75.

How to Write Better Business Letters, Earle A. Buckley, McGraw-Hill, New York, 1957, $5.00.

How to Write Successful Business Letters in 15 Days, John P. Reibel, Prentice-Hall, Englewood Cliffs, N.J., 1953, $4.95.

The KRC Portfolio of Model Fund-Raising Letters, KRC Associates, 105 Mamaroneck Avenue, Mamaroneck, New York 10543, 1972, $30.00.

Make Yourself Clear!, John O. Morris, McGraw-Hill, New York, 1972, $8.95.

Plain Letters, Mona Sheppard, Simon & Schuster, New York, 1960, $4.50.

Plain Letters, Mona Sheppard, U.S. Govt. Printing Office, Washington, D.C., 30¢.

The Robert Collier Letter Book, Robert Collier, Prentice-Hall, Englewood Cliffs, N.J., 1950, (sixth edition), $12.95.

Sizzlemanship—New Tested Selling Sentences, Elmer Wheeler, Prentice-Hall, Englewood Cliffs, N.J., 1940, $4.95.

Ten Commandments for Writing Letters That Get Results, John P. Reibel and Donald R. Robert, Printers' Ink, New London, Conn., 1957, $6.00.

Tested Sentences that Sell, Elmer Wheeler, Prentice-Hall, Englewood Cliffs, N.J., 1937, $4.95.

Word Magic, Elmer Wheeler, Prentice-Hall, Englewood Cliffs, N.J., 1939.

Words on Target, Sue Nichols, John Knox Press, Richmond, Va., 1963, $2.45.

MOTIVATION AND PERSUASION

The Art of Negotiating, Gerald I. Nierenberg, Cornerstone Library, 1971, $1.95.

The Difficult Art of Giving; The Epic of Alan Gregg, Wilder Penfield, Little Brown & Company, 200 West Street, Waltham, Mass. 02154, 1967, $7.95.

"Donor Needs," Paul H. Davis, *Journal of Higher Education*, 40:231-4, (March, 1969).

Getting Along with Difficult People, Frederich Schmitt (Erich R. Schultz, translated from German), Fortress, 1970, $2.50.

Getting Through to People, Jesse S. Nirenberg, Prentice-Hall, Englewood Cliffs, N.J., 1970, $2.45.

How to Succeed with Committees, David M. Church, Motivation, Inc., P.O. Box 4695, Stamford, Conn. 06907, 1966, $5.95.

How to Succeed with Volunteers, David M. Church. National Public Relations Council for Health & Welfare Service, 419 Park Avenue South, New York, N.Y. 10016, 1962, $1.25.

How to Talk with People, Lee, Irving J., New York: Harper and Row, 1952, 176 pp.

Innovation in Marketing, Theodore Levitt. London: Pan Books Ltd., 1962, $2.00.

Learning to Give, K. Russell and J. Tooke, Pergamon, 1968, $5.50.

Mannerisms of Speech and Gestures in Everyday Life, Sandor S. Feldman, International Universities Press, 1959.

Man's Concern for His Fellow Man, Arnaud C. Marts. W. F. Humphrey Press, Inc., Geneva, New York, 1961, $2.00.

The Marketing Mode, Theodore Levitt. New York: McGraw-Hill Book Co., New York, 1969, $9.25.

Meaning of Gifts, Paul Tournier, John Knox, Richmond, Va., 1963, $2.50.

The Volunteer Board Member in Philanthropy, National Information Bureau, Inc., 305 East 45th Street, New York, N.Y. 10017, 1968, $1.00.

Persuade and Provide, Michael Newton and Scott Hatley. Associated Councils of the Arts, 1564 Broadway, New York, N.Y. 10036, 1970, $7.50.

Practical Business Psychology, Donal A. & Eleanor Laird, McGraw-Hill, New York, 1961, $8.00, (third edition).

The Rich, Are They Different?, George G. Kirstein. Houghton Mifflin Co., 2 Park Street, Boston, Mass. 02122, 1968, $5.95.

Sense and Nonsense: A Study in Human Communication, Alfred Fleishman, International Society for General Semantics, San Francisco, 1971, $2.00.

Stewardship in Contemporary Theology, T. K. Thompson (ed.), Association Press, 291 Broadway, New York, N.Y. 10007, 1960, $4.95.

Visual Persuasion, Stephen Baker, McGraw-Hill, New York, 1961, $13.50.

The Volunteers: Means and Ends in a National Organization, David L. Sills, The Free Press of Glencoe, New York, 1957.

Why People Give, Martin E. Carlson. National Council of Churches, 475 Riverside Drive, New York, N.Y. 10027, 1968, $1.25.

Worldly Goods, James Gollin, Random House, New York, 1971, $8.95.

PHILANTHROPY

American Philanthropy, Robert H. Bremmer, University of Chicago Press, 11030 S. Langly, Chicago, Ill. 60628, 1960, $5.00 ($1.95 in paper back).

American Philanthropy Abroad, Merle Curti. Rutgers University Press, 30 College Avenue, New Brunswick, N.J. 08903, 1963, $12.50.

America's Needs and Resources, Dewhurst and Associates. 20th Century Fund, 41 East 70th Street, New York, N.Y. 10021, 1955, $12.00.

American Welfare, DeGrazia and Gurr. NYU Press, New York University, Washington Square, New York, N.Y. 10003, 1961, $7.50.

A Winner in the American Tradition (biography), Paul C. Carter & Arnaud Cartwright Marts. Algonquin Press, 380 Lexington Avenue, New York, N.Y. 10017, 1970, $5.00.

"Can Our Nonprofit Institutions Survive?", *Institutional Investor*. (special issue, August, 1972) Kennington Publishing Corp., 140 Cedar St., N.Y., N.Y. 10006 (Subscriptions not available to anyone outside the securities field).

The Catholic Church & Social Welfare, Marguerita T. Boylan. Greenwich Book Publishers, 282 Seventh Avenue, New York, N.Y. 10001, 1961, $5.00.

Changing Position of Philanthropy in the American Economy (Occasional Paper #107), Frank G. Dickinson, National Bureau of Economic Research, 1970, $6.00.

Community Chest: A Case Study in Philanthropy, John R. Seeley and others. University of Toronto Press, Toronto, Ontario, Canada, 1957, $7.50.

Fund Raising in the United States: Its Role in America's Philanthropy, Scott M. Cutlip, Rutgers University Press, 1965, $12.50.

The Generosity of Americans, Arnaud C. Marts, Prentice-Hall, Englewood Cliffs, N.J., $5.95.

History and Role of Philanthropy in American Society, Vol. 105 No. 2, American Philosophical Society, Proceedings of. APS, 104 South 5th Street, Philadelphia, Pa. 19106, 1961, $1.00.

Only by Public Consent, L. L. L. Golden. Howthorn Books, Inc., 70 Fifth Avenue, N.Y., 10011, 1968, $7.95.

Philanthropic Giving, F. Emerson Andrews, Russell Sage, 1950, $7.50.

Philanthropy and Public Policy, Frank G. Dickinson. National Bureau of Economic Research, Inc., 261 Madison Avenue, New York, N.Y. 10016, 1962, $3.50.

Philanthropy in England, 1480-1660, W. D. Jordan. Russell Sage Foundation, 230 Park Avenue, N.Y. 10017, 1959, $6.00.

Planning for Better Hospital Care, Eli and Rogatz Ginsburg. Kings

Crown Press, Columbia University, 440 West 110th Street, New York, N.Y. 10026, 1961, $5.00.

Welfare in America, Vaughn Davis Bornet, University of Oklahoma Press, University of Oklahoma, Norman, Okla. 73069, 1960, $4.95.

PUBLIC RELATIONS AND MEETINGS

Apollo Handbook of Practical Public Relations, Alexander B. Adams, Apollo Editions, Thomas Y. Crowell Company, New York, 1970, $2.65.

Covers, Covers, Covers, American Alumni Council, Washington, D.C., $2.50.

Effective Public Relations, Scott M. Cutlip and Allen H. Center, Prentice-Hall, Englewood Cliffs, New Jersey, 1971.

Guide to Conducting Meetings, J. E. Baird, Abingdon, 1965, 75¢.

Handbook of Special Events for Nonprofit Organizations, Edwin R. Leibert and Bernice E. Sheldon, Association Press, New York, N.Y. 10007, 1972, $12.95.

Hospital Public Relations Today, Alden Mills, Physicians Record Company, Berwyn, Illinois, 1964.

How to Conduct a Meeting, J. Q. Tilson, Oceana, 1950, 75¢.

How to Plan and Conduct Workshops and Conferences, R. Bechard, Association Press, 291 Broadway, New York, New York 10017.

How to Produce an Effective Newsletter, Richard Hodgson, American Marketing Services, Waltham, Mass., 1960, $1.00.

"An Information Campaign That Changed Community Attitudes," Dorothy F. Doughlas, et al, *Journalism Quarterly*, Vol. 47, Autumn, 1970.

Modern Rules of Order, L. S. Cushing, Fawcett World, 1969, 75¢.

Practical Publicity: A Handbook for Public and Private Workers, Herbert Jacobs, McGraw-Hill, 1964, $6.50.

The Public Relations Committee, David M. Church. National Public Relations Council for Health & Welfare Services, 419 Park Avenue S, New York 10016, 1949, $1.00.

"Public Relations for Religion and Religious Groups," Stewart Harral, *Public Relations Handbook*, Prentice-Hall, Inc., Englewood Cliffs, New Jersey, 1962, 369-77.

Public Relations in Health and Welfare, Frances Schmidt & Harold N. Weiner. Columbia University Press, 136 South Broadway, Irving-on-Hudson, N.Y. 10533, 1966, $6.50.

Public Relations for Social Agencies, Harold P. Levy, Harper & Row, New York, N.Y., 1956.

Successful Conference and Discussion Techniques, H. P. Zelko, McGraw-Hill, 1957, $2.75.

SELLING

Guideposts for Effective Salesmanship, Robert R. Blake & Jane Srygley Mouton, Playboy Press, Chicago, 1970, $1.25.

How to Sell Intangibles, Abbot P. Smith, Prentice-Hall, Englewood Cliffs, N.J., 1958, $4.95.

Profitable Showmanship, Kenneth Goode & Zenn Kaufman, Prentice-Hall, Englewood Cliffs, N.J., 1939.

Sales Promotions That Get Results, Howard M. Turner, McGraw-Hill, New York, N.Y., 1959, $6.95.

Successful Low Pressure Salesmanship, Edward Berman, Zerweck-Berman, Inc., Box 399, Media, Pa. 19063, $1.95.